23 Ready-To-Go Lesson Plans
SOCIAL STUDIES
GRADE 2

D1417745

What Are Lifesaver Lessons®?

Lifesaver Lessons® are well-planned, easy-to-implement, curriculum-based lessons. Each lesson contains a complete materials list, step-by-step instructions, a reproducible activity or pattern, and several extension activities.

How Do I Use A Lifesaver Lessons® Unit?

Each Lifesaver Lesson is designed to decrease your preparation time and increase the amount of quality teaching time with your students. These lessons are great for introducing or reinforcing new concepts. Use the handy list below to see what types of materials to gather. After completing a lesson, be sure to check out the fun-filled extension activities.

What Materials Will I Need?

Most of the materials for each lesson can be easily found in your classroom or school. Check the list of materials below for any items you may need to gather or purchase.

- crayons
- markers
- assorted colors of chalk
- scissors
- glue
- tape
- rulers
- writing paper
- chart paper
- duplicating paper

- drawing paper
- stapler
- bulletin-board paper
- sticky notes
- construction paper
- index cards
- United States map
- world map
- globe
- medium-size box

- poster board
- calendar
- brads
- shopping bag
- plastic bag

- markers (such as beans or pennies)
- magazine pictures
- car keys

Project Editor:
Mary Lester

Contributing Editor:
Darcy Brown

Writers:
Darcy Brown, Heather Godwin, Cynthia Holcomb,
Susie Kapaun, Laura Mihalenko, Melanie Miller,
Vicki Mockaitis, Valarie Wood Smith

Artists:
Cathy Spangler Bruce, Teresa R. Davidson, Nick Greenwood,
Clevell Harris, Theresa Lewis, Rob Mayworth, Kimberly
Richard, Rebecca Saunders, Barry Slate, Donna K. Teal

Cover Artist:
Kimberly Richard

World Map

Lifesaver Lessons®

Table Of Contents

Communities

The Family 3

Community Helpers 7

Urban, Suburban, And Rural Settings 11

Government & Citizenship

Rules In A Neighborhood 15

Good Neighborhood Citizens 19

Neighborhood Rights 23

Democratic Decision Making 27

U.S. Symbols 31

Map Skills

Maps And Globes 35

Cardinal Directions 39

Reading A Map Key 43

Geographic Terms 47

Our Neighbors

Neighborhoods Around The World 51

Holidays From Different Cultures 55

History

Timeline Of U.S. Holidays 59

Comparing Today With The Past 63

Historical Figures 67

Economics

Wants And Needs 71

Supply And Demand 75

Goods And Services 79

Producers And Consumers 83

Money As A Means Of Exchange 87

Division Of Labor 91

Answer Keys 95

Management Checklist 96

©1999 by THE EDUCATION CENTER, INC.
All rights reserved.
ISBN #1-56234-302-5

Manufactured in the United States
10 9 8 7 6 5 4 3 2 1

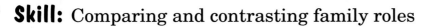

All In The Family

*Teach youngsters that no matter the size or age,
family members help each other in many different ways!*

Skill: Comparing and contrasting family roles

Estimated Lesson Time: 30 minutes

Teacher Preparation:
1. Duplicate page 5 for each student.
2. On a sheet of bulletin-board paper, draw and label a bar graph similar to the one shown on page 4.

Materials:
1 copy of page 5 per student
labeled bar graph
1 sticky note per student

Background Information:
Family members
- keep homes clean and tidy
- prepare meals
- repair things when necessary
- help each other learn
- celebrate together
- take care of each other when someone is sick or hurt
- take care of pets
- show each other how much they care

Introducing The Lesson:

Tell students that today is Family Day in social studies. Although families will not actually be in the classroom, they will be an important part of the lesson.

Steps:

1. Share the Background Information on page 3. Ask each student to volunteer something about her role as a family member.

2. Tell students that they are going to create a bar graph that shows the different roles of their family members. Distribute a sticky note to each child and instruct her to write her name on it.

3. Display the prepared bar graph. Explain that you are going to ask questions about family roles. Here are some sample questions:
   —Who feeds the pets in your family?
   —Who cooks the meals?
   —Who washes the dishes?
   —Who does the laundry?
   —Who takes out the trash?
   —Who works on the car?
   —Who does most of the shopping?

4. Ask the class a question such as one of those listed above. To answer it, have each student place her sticky note on the corresponding column of the graph.

5. Discuss the resulting graph. Then redistribute the sticky notes and repeat step 3, asking a different question.

6. Once youngsters understand the concept of family roles, distribute a copy of page 5 to each student. Review the directions; then have her complete the page independently.

7. Challenge students to complete the Bonus Box activity.

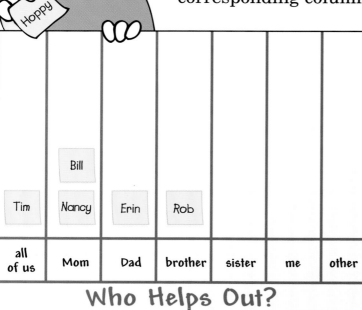

all of us	Mom	Dad	brother	sister	me	other
Tim	Bill					
	Nancy	Erin	Rob			

Who Helps Out?

Comparing and contrasting family roles

All In The Family

Draw a picture of yourself in this frame.
Write about two ways you help your family.

1. _____

_____

_____

_____

2. _____

_____

_____

_____

Draw a picture of another family member in
this frame.
Write about two ways that person helps
your family.

1. _____

_____

_____

_____

2. _____

_____

_____

_____

Bonus Box: On the back of this paper, list the name of another family
member. Draw a picture that illustrates how he or she helps your family.

(5)

How To Extend The Lesson:

- Put creative-writing skills to work with this inventive assignment. Ask each student to imagine that he could add one more relative to his family. Encourage him to describe and name the new family member, explain the reasons for wanting him or her in the family, and tell about the roles he or she would have. If desired, have each student draw a picture to accompany his writing assignment.

- Invite students to share a special family memory with the class. In advance, send a note home asking family members to discuss a favorite memory. Encourage each family to contribute a photograph, a written account, a souvenir, or some other memento of the occasion. Provide a special show-and-tell time for each student to share her family memory with her classmates.

- Use this bulletin-board project to reinforce the different and special types of families. Draw a large apartment-shaped building on a large sheet of bulletin-board paper; then cut out a large window for each student. Have each child draw a picture of her family to tape behind a window. Challenge each student to tell about the similarities and differences of the families pictured.

Taking Care Of The Community

Introduce your students to the people who take care of their community with these class-created cards.

Skill: Analyzing the roles of different community helpers

Estimated Lesson Time: 45 minutes

Teacher Preparation:
Duplicate one copy of page 9 onto white construction paper for each student.

Materials:
1 white construction-paper copy of page 9 for each student
glue
crayons

Background Information:
- A *community* is any group living in the same area or having interests and work in common.
- Communities provide services for the people who live in them.
- Community governments make sure that community services run smoothly.
- Communities choose people to run different services in the community.
- The police and fire departments are examples of two types of community service.
- Some examples of community helpers include
  —firefighter
  —police officer
  —teacher
  —nurse
  —doctor
  —paramedic
  —sanitation worker
  —bus driver
  —veterinarian
  —construction worker

Introducing The Lesson:

Write "community helper" on the chalkboard. Have students name several community helpers. List students' responses on the board. Then challenge the class to name the different jobs each community helper performs.

Steps:

1. Remind students that community helpers perform different jobs to take care of the community. Then share the Background Information on page 7.

2. Distribute a copy of page 9 to each child.

3. Assign each child a different community helper from the list on page 7. (Some helpers may be assigned to more than one student.)

4. Instruct each student to write the name of his community helper on the provided line on page 9. Then have him draw a picture of his helper in the box.

5. Next direct each youngster to complete the information about his community helper on the right side of his paper.

6. Then, to complete the project, instruct each student to fold his paper along the dotted line and glue the two sides together.

7. Invite students to share their community helper cards with their classmates. Then collect the cards and place them at a center for further investigation.

Name: _____

Community Helper:

This community helper is _____

This community helper works to
___ keep us healthy.
___ keep us safe.
___ give us transportation.
___ help us learn.
___ give us goods.
___ provide us with a service.

This community helper works
___ inside only.
___ outside only.
___ both inside and outside.

This community helper works
___ in the daytime only.
___ at night only.
___ both day and night.

The place where this community helper works is _____

The special equipment this community helper uses is _____

This community helper is important to the community because _____

How To Extend The Lesson:

- Distribute a different community helper card to each student. Ask youngsters to group the helpers by types of jobs, places of work, or people they help.

- Invite some helpers in your community to your classroom to tell about their jobs. Before each visit, challenge each youngster to write five questions to ask the helper about her job. Then have the students ask the community helper their questions during her visit.

- Take a walking field trip or a bus ride around your community. Encourage students to take note of all the helpers found throughout the trip. If desired, have students keep a tally of the helpers found in each workplace. Then compile the information into a bar graph after the trip.

- Have each student think of which community helper's job she might like to have as a career in the future. Challenge the student to draw a picture of herself working as her selected community helper. Then ask the student to write about the jobs she would perform for the community. Invite students to share their creations with the class. Then, if desired, display the papers on a bulletin board titled "Future Community Helpers."

When I am grown-up, I will be a teacher. I will teach grade school. I will help students be better learners.

I am going to be a great doctor when I grow up. I will make sick people well. I will take care of sick children.

Analyzing the roles of different community helpers

What's It Like?

Have your students visit three types of communities and discover the importance of each one.

Skill: Comparing and contrasting urban, suburban, and rural settings

Estimated Lesson Time: 45 minutes

Teacher Preparation:

1. Duplicate page 13 for each student.
2. Divide a sheet of chart paper into three columns. Label the first column "Urban," the middle column "Suburban," and the last column "Rural." Post the chart in a prominent location.
3. Cut three pictures from a magazine—an urban, a suburban, and a rural setting.

Materials:

1 copy of page 13 per student
labeled chart
3 magazine pictures
crayons
scissors
glue

Background Information:

- Urban setting—a large city community
- Suburban setting—a community that is near a city
- Rural setting—a community that is near forests or farms
- Many people live in cities (urban settings). There are a lot of schools, stores, and different kinds of jobs. Cities can be very crowded and noisy. Sometimes there is a lot of traffic in a city.
- Suburbs are communities near large cities. They have their own schools and business centers. People often move to the suburbs because they do not want to live in large cities.
- Most of the people who live in rural settings know one another. These community members may farm or raise animals for food.

Introducing The Lesson:

Share the three magazine pictures with students. Ask students to point out the picture that most looks like their community and tell why.

Steps:

1. Point to the picture of the urban setting and ask students to name things they may find in this type of community. Record their responses on the chart under the column labeled "Urban." (See the examples below.)

2. Repeat the process with each of the remaining magazine pictures, recording student responses in the appropriate columns.

3. Discuss with students the Background Information on page 11. Then review the students' community responses on the chart paper. Referring to each item on the list of responses, have students verify that each is in the appropriate column.

4. Distribute a copy of page 13 to each student. Read the directions together and have students complete the page independently. Challenge students to complete the Bonus Box activity.

Urban	Suburban	Rural
crowded streets	houses in neighborhoods	lots of land
tall buildings	people mowing yards	farms
many people	children at school	trees
lots of cars	shopping mall	few cars
traffic		country roads
many stores		

Name _____

What's It Like?

Color and cut out the pictures. Glue each picture in the correct box.
Then write about each setting on the lines.

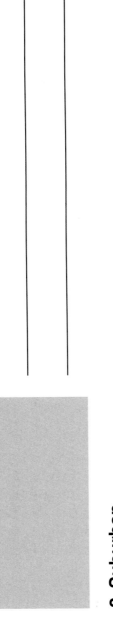

1. Urban

2. Suburban

3. Rural

Bonus Box: In which place would you most like to live? On the back of this paper, write why you would live in that type of setting.

How To Extend The Lesson:

- Put creative talents to work as students make a class chapter book of urban, suburban, and rural areas. Have each student cut out a picture of either an urban, suburban, or rural setting from a discarded magazine. (You may wish to assign settings so that the areas are evenly distributed.) Direct him to glue his picture to a sheet of construction paper. Instruct him to write a few sentences to accompany his picture. Then have students help categorize the completed pictures into urban, suburban, or rural settings. Place a labeled divider page ("Urban," "Suburban", or "Rural") between each section before binding the pages into a class booklet.

- Have students work in small groups to develop a community newsletter. To begin, provide each group with a description of a real or imaginary community (in an urban, suburban, or rural setting). Instruct students to design newsletters featuring articles related to their assigned communities. Challenge each group to include items such as upcoming community events, sales ads, school activities, and housing information. Encourage students to include headlines, illustrations, and captions for each article. Display the completed newsletters for all to enjoy!

- Have each student select the kind of community in which she would prefer to live—an urban, suburban, or rural area. Provide students with a supply of discarded magazines. Direct each youngster to cut out pictures that represent the type of community she chose. Then have the student glue her pictures to a tagboard house shape to make a collage. Provide time for each student to share her reasons for choosing her selected area. Then display the projects on a bulletin board titled "Home, Sweet Homes."

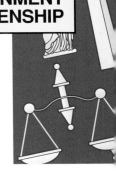

Best Neighborhood Behaviors

What's the word around the neighborhood? Conduct counts!
Review the shoulds and shouldn'ts of neighborly behavior.

Skill: Identifying neighborhood rules

Estimated Lesson Time: 30 minutes

Teacher Preparation:
Duplicate page 17 ont~~... P 15 ld rules ...~~per for each student.

Materials:
1 white construction-p⎯
   of page 17 per stud⎯
1 additional sheet of ⎯⎯⎯
   construction paper per student
scissors
glue
crayons

Background Information:
A neighborhood has many kinds of rules. For example, parks have rules to help us get along. Schools have rules that keep order, so that everyone can learn. There are even rules to protect us when we cross the street. Rules help keep a neighborhood safe, healthy, and free from problems.

Introducing The Lesson:

Tell students that instead of having a lesson, they are going to play a game. Ask a student volunteer to come to the board and play a game of tic-tac-toe with you. Invite the student to make the first move. As she begins to take her turn, take your turn at the same time. Continue playing the game, making several mistakes, such as taking two turns in a row, erasing one of the student's marks, and changing one of your marks from *X* to *O*.

Steps:

1. After the game, ask students to explain why things didn't go smoothly. Confirm that there is a set of rules that both players should follow to ensure that the game is played fairly.

2. Next ask students to identify some other instances in which there are rules to follow. Reinforce answers such as fire drills, library visits, bike riding, and crossing streets.

3. Inform students that there are also certain rules that we follow in our neighborhoods. Share the Background Information on page 15 with your students. Then ask them to identify several neighborhood rules and explain the reasons for them.

4. Distribute a copy of page 17 and one sheet of white construction paper to each student. Instruct each youngster to color the picture and trim the pattern along the bold lines. Next have him cut his pattern along the dotted lines to create doors that open outward. Then direct the student to draw a line of glue around the border of the pattern page and place it atop the sheet of white construction paper, making sure the doors are not glued down. (See the illustration below.)

5. Instruct each child to list five neighborhood rules on the white paper behind his doors. Then have him decorate the back of each door with illustrations of people in his neighborhood.

6. Collect the projects and display them on a bulletin board titled "Best Neighborhood Behaviors!"

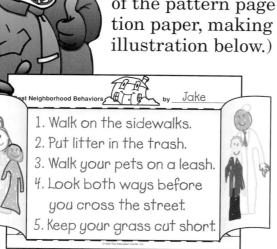

Best Neighborhood Behaviors by Jake
1. Walk on the sidewalks.
2. Put litter in the trash.
3. Walk your pets on a leash.
4. Look both ways before you cross the street.
5. Keep your grass cut short.

Best Neighborhood Behaviors

by _____

17 white construction

How To Extend The Lesson:

- Have students evaluate the existing rules for school activities such as going to the library, eating in the cafeteria, handling science equipment, or playing on the playground. Ask them to discuss the reasons for the current rules, whether or not they seem fair, and if additional rules need to be enforced. If desired, challenge each student to write and then illustrate another rule for the activity.

- Personalize the importance of rules by asking each child to imagine that he is going to entertain a small child in his room while his parents have visitors. Ask him to make a list of rules for playing in his room and with his toys. Remind him that rules need to be fair as well as protective!

- Have students illustrate important neighborhood rules by having each child create a minibook. Provide each student with five unlined index cards and crayons. Instruct her to use four of the cards to draw and label pictures that reinforce neighborhood rules. Next have her create a cover from the remaining index card. Help the student staple her completed cards together to make a minibook. Then display the completed projects in your reading center to reinforce appropriate neighborhood behavior.

- Share with your students the book *Officer Buckle And Gloria* by Peggy Rathmann (Scholastic Inc., 1995). In this tale, a police officer with a wealth of safety tips finds a perfect (and four-legged!) partner to interest children in his safety campaign. After the story, invite a police officer to speak to your students about neighborhood safety. Wrap up his visit by challenging small groups of students to each make a poster showing safety both during and after school.

Always walk with a buddy.

Look both ways before you cross the street.

Hello, Good Neighbor!

Explore good citizenship with these neighborly activities.

Skill: Identifying characteristics of neighborhood citizenship

Estimated Lesson Time: 45 minutes

Teacher Preparation:

1. Duplicate page 21 onto white construction paper for each student.
2. Program a set of ind[...]ng. (See page 20 for examples.)

p19 Citizenship

Materials:

1 white construction-pap[...] each student
programmed index cards
scissors
glue

Howdy, neighbor!

Background Information:

Good citizens are people who

- respect others
- respect property
- obey rules and laws
- help others
- work together

Introducing The Lesson:

Tell students that they will work together in groups to role-play some situations that might happen in a neighborhood. Explain that you will give each group a card telling about the situation. The group members will discuss what good neighbors would say and do in that situation; then they will act it out in front of the class.

Steps:

1. Organize students into groups of two or three. Distribute a programmed card to each group. (Examples are shown below.) Allow time for students to discuss and plan their role-play situation. Then have students return to their seats to watch each group act out good neighborhood citizenship.

2. Next discuss the scene performed by each group. Have students point out the examples of good citizenship shown by each group. Then review the characteristics of good citizenship listed in the Background Information shown on page 19.

3. Distribute a copy of page 21 to each student. Review the directions; then have each child complete her page independently.

4. Invite students to display their projects on a countertop in the classroom.

A young child falls off his bike. He is crying for his mother.

A neighbor is sick in bed. You know it is her birthday.

A neighbor has a large sack of groceries. She can't open the door to her house.

A neighbor has gone on a trip. The wind blows over the flowerpots on his porch.

Two children see another child at the park. He is writing his name on a bench.

You see a strange car in the neighborhood. It keeps driving slowly up and down your street.

Identifying characteristics of neighborhood citizenship

Hello, Good Neighbor!

Color the cards and the houses.
Cut out the houses on the bold line and the picture cards on the dotted lines.
Read each card and glue to the correct house in the shaded area.
Then draw two more pictures for each house. Write about each picture.
Fold the completed project along the center line.

Good Neighbors Don't...   ### Good Neighbors Do...

fold

follow rules	act unkindly	help each other	litter
damage property	work together	respect others	let pets run loose

How To Extend The Lesson:

- Have each student interview family members to find out how they show good neighborhood citizenship. Provide time for students to share their findings. Then have each student draw and label an illustration of her family demonstrating good neighborhood citizenship. Compile the completed drawings into a class booklet titled "Hello, Good Neighbor!"

- Challenge students to cut out examples from discarded magazines of different types of neighborhoods and people showing neighborly acts. Have students glue their pictures in collage fashion to a large piece of bulletin-board paper. Mount the completed collage to a large wall; then add the title "Welcome To The Neighborhood!"

- Reinforce neighborly relations with this thank-you note project. Invite each child to tell about a person in the community who has demonstrated neighborhood citizenship. Then instruct each youngster to fold a sheet of construction paper in half to make a card. Next have him write a note of gratitude to this person. Then invite him to decorate his card as desired. Encourage each child to hand-deliver his note of appreciation.

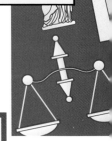

Neighborhood Know-How!

*Help your students learn to be good neighbors
and use their rights responsibly.*

Skill: Understanding neighborhood rights and responsibilities

Estimated Lesson Time: 30 minutes

Teacher Preparation:
Duplicate page 25 for each student.

Materials:
1 copy of page 25 for ea~~ch stu~~dent
crayons

Rights   p23

Background Information:
Neighborhood responsibilities include the following:
- helping to keep the neighborhood clean
- keeping noise at an appropriate level
- following safety rules
- being considerate of other people's feelings
- respecting other people's privacy
- respecting other people's property

Introducing The Lesson:

Write the word *neighbor* on the chalkboard. Ask each student to think of a good neighbor who lives near him. Challenge him to think about the characteristics that make this person a good neighbor.

Steps:

1. Encourage each student to talk about the characteristics of a good neighbor. Write students' responses on the chalkboard.

2. Explain that all neighbors have rights and with these rights come responsibilities. For example, neighbors have the right to live in a clean community, so all neighbors are responsible for putting their trash in its proper place. Another example is that people have the right to be safe, so all neighbors need to be responsible and follow safety rules.

3. Ask students to give more examples of neighborhood rights and responsibilities. Guide students to include the responsibilities listed in the Background Information on page 23.

4. Distribute crayons and a copy of page 25 to each student. Instruct him to illustrate and write about a responsible neighborhood behavior.

5. Invite each student to share his completed work with the class.

6. If desired, display their work on a bulletin board or compile them into a class booklet.

He is stopping his car at a stop sign. This is responsible because he is being careful of others.

He is playing his boombox quietly. He is being responsible by not disturbing his neighbors with loud music.

Neighborhood Know-How!

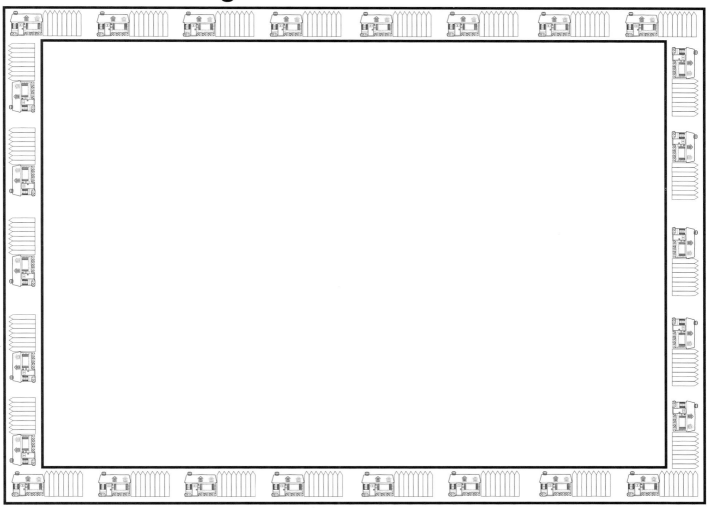

All neighbors have rights. With these rights come responsibilities.
Draw a picture of a responsible neighbor.

This neighbor is being responsible because _____

_____

_____

_____

_____

_____

_____

How To Extend The Lesson:

- Provide time for students to share examples of how they have been responsible neighbors and the rights that they protect by their actions. Create a newspaper titled "The Neighborhood News." Have students write or dictate articles about protecting rights in the neighborhood through responsible actions.

- Incorporate writing skills by having each youngster describe the rights and responsibilities that are evident in his neighborhood. If some responsibilities are not met, encourage each student to think of ways that he could improve the situation.

- For a truly hands-on activity, have students make these helping hand puppets. Have each youngster trace his hand on a piece of construction paper and cut the pattern out. Next have him draw a small self-portrait on the palm of his cutout. Then, on each finger, have him write a different way that he acts responsibly in his neighborhood. To complete the project, have each youngster glue his cutout to a craft stick as shown. Invite students to sit in a circle and use their puppets to describe neighborhood rights and responsibilities.

I play quietly.
I am polite.
I don't litter.
I am safe.
I share.

Let's Vote!

Youngsters will cast votes of approval for this democratic activity!

Skill: Participating in the democratic process

Estimated Lesson Time: 30 minutes

Teacher Preparation:
1. Duplicate page 29 for each student.
2. Determine issues to be put to a vote. (See list of suggestions below.)

Materials:
1 copy of page 29 for each student
chalk or dry-erase markers in
   assorted colors

Background Information:
Registration is the process by which a person has his or her name added to a list of qualified voters. When a person wants to vote, an official checks the voter's name against the list of qualified voters.

Possible Classroom Voting Issues
- The signal to be used for asking a question
- The method of lining up for the day
- The game to play at recess
- The color of crayon to be used in checking papers

Introducing The Lesson:

Ask students to think of a time when they may have had to make a decision at home—like what to eat for dinner or what program to watch on television. Then ask each student to think of how her decision might have been affected if another family member did not make the same decision.

Steps:

1. Inform students that each person has a chance to make her opinion known by putting an issue to a vote. The choice with the most votes—the *majority*—wins.

2. Tell students that you would like to use a different color of chalk (or dry-erase marker) during the lesson. Display three different colors of chalk. Ask each student to raise her hand to vote for the color of her choice. Tally students' votes on the board.

3. Ask students to determine which color wins the election.

4. Explain the practice of voter registration (see Background Information on page 27) and distribute a copy of page 29 to each student. Have her cut out the voter registration card (the top portion of the page), setting aside the tally sheet (the bottom portion of the page). Then direct the student to fill in the information on her registration card.

5. Announce the topic of the next election. Write the choices to be voted upon at the top of the chalkboard. Then have each student cut out her tally sheet and fill in the information.

6. Have each student, in turn, show you her voter registration card and cast a vote by putting her initials beneath her choice on the chalkboard.

7. Have each youngster tally the results on her sheet as you do the same on the board. Then tell which choice gets the majority of votes and announce the winner of the election.

Voter Registration Card

Name _____

Address _____

_____

_____

Date Of Birth_____

Signature _____

Tally Sheet

Election Time

I VOTED!

Topic:_____

Choices: **Tally:**

1. _____

2. _____

3. _____

4. _____

The majority voted for_____.

How To Extend The Lesson:

• Integrate a little graphing practice into your election results. After tallying the results of each election, draw a reusable bar graph on the chalkboard or a sheet of chart paper. Have each child place a mark on the graph to show how she voted. Then ask student volunteers to make observations about the resulting information.

• Arrange for a guest speaker from the voter registration office to visit your classroom. Have the speaker explain the registration process, including the use of ballots. If possible, have her show examples of ballots that have been used in previous elections. Then invite her to hold a mock election for students to participate in.

• Use the democratic process to create an interest in literature. At the beginning of the week, place three or four books in your reading center. Explain that you will read one of the books to the class on Friday. Invite the students to examine the books throughout the week. On Friday, write the title of each book on the chalkboard. Instruct each student to make a campaign poster or button to promote her preference. After displaying the projects, distribute a slip of paper to each student. Have her vote for one book by writing its title on her slip of paper. Collect the slips. Count each vote by making a tally mark on the chalkboard beside the corresponding title. Conclude the election by reading the winning book to the class.

Let's Get Patriotic!

*Put pizzazz into the study of patriotic symbols
with this fun-and-games lesson.*

Skill: Identifying patriotic symbols

Estimated Lesson Time: 30 minutes

Teacher Preparation:
Duplicate page 33 for each student.

Materials:
1 copy of page 33 per student
1 extra copy of page 33
9 markers (counters, dried beans, or
  pennies) per student
plastic bag
scissors
glue

Background Information:

Patriotic symbols show that Americans are proud of their country. Many of the symbols remind us of our early struggles to be free. Other symbols remind us of the people who have helped to make our nation a great place to live.

bald eagle: our national bird, a symbol of freedom and power
"The Star-Spangled Banner": our national anthem, a patriotic song about our country
American flag: a symbol with a stripe for each original colony and a star for each state
Liberty Bell: the bell that rang out to announce our country's freedom
Pledge of Allegiance: our promise to be loyal to our country
Uncle Sam: a cartoon symbol dressed in patriotic red, white, and blue; his initials are U.S.
fireworks: lit on Independence Day to show our patriotic spirit
White House: where the president and his family live in Washington, DC
Statue of Liberty: one of the best known U.S. symbols; the statue is in New York Harbor

Introducing The Lesson:

Welcome students to a new game show called "Let's Get Patriotic!" Introduce yourself as the host, who will help the class earn patriotic points. After a certain number of patriotic points have been earned, students will then play a lotto version of the game.

Steps:

1. To prepare for the game show, write the symbol words (without the definitions) from the Background Information (page 31) on the chalkboard. To play, read aloud a definition and ask students to identify its matching symbol. If a word is correctly identified, make a tally mark (patriotic point) on the board. Continue until all symbols have been defined.

2. Challenge the class to a bonus round. Select a symbol from the list and ask students to define it. Award a bonus point for each correct definition. (Provide the opportunity for all students to participate.)

3. Tell students that they are ready to play another version of the game to help them remember these patriotic symbols. Distribute a copy of page 33 to each student. Instruct him to cut out the patriotic symbols and randomly glue them onto his lotto board.

4. As students are preparing their gameboards, cut apart the symbols from the extra copy of page 33. Store the pieces in a plastic bag.

5. Next distribute nine gameboard markers to each student. Then draw a patriotic symbol from your bag. Direct each student to cover the matching symbol on his card with a marker. Then draw another symbol from the bag. The first student to get three in a row wins the game. If desired, have the winner become the caller for another round of play.

6. Vary the game by having students try to cover their four corners, fill in the middle row, or form an *X* with their marker pieces.

7. Challenge students to complete the Bonus Box activity.

Name _____

Bald
Eagle

National Anthem

Pledge
of
Allegiance

Fireworks

Liberty Bell

American
Flag

Statue of
Liberty

Uncle
Sam

White House

Let's Get Patriotic!

Cut out each patriotic symbol.
Mix up the cards.
Then glue each one onto the gameboard.

JULY 2

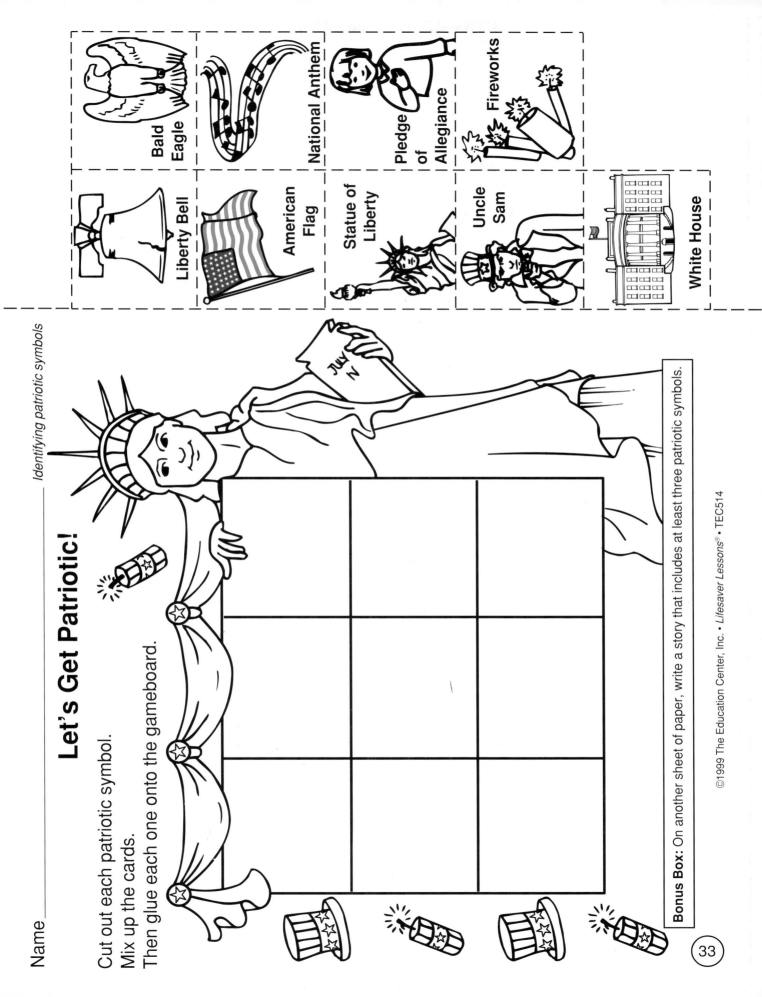

Bonus Box: On another sheet of paper, write a story that includes at least three patriotic symbols.

33

How To Extend The Lesson:

- Encourage national pride by having students make patriotic pennants. Distribute markers and a triangular construction-paper pennant to each child. Instruct her to create a pennant with words or symbols to show pride in our country. Provide time for youngsters to share their pennants. Then display the banners in the classroom for a show of patriotic pizzazz!

- Have each student select a patriotic symbol of America, such as the flag or the Liberty Bell. Instruct him to imagine that he is "interviewing" the symbol for a newspaper article about the way it represents America. Have him add a drawing of the symbol to his writing assignment. Provide time for volunteers to share their articles with the class.

- Have each student conduct a home survey to find out which patriotic symbol is especially meaningful to family members. Discuss the outcomes of the surveys in class. Then, if desired, make a class pictograph to show which symbols were selected most often.

- Put creative skills to work as you have students create a "museum" of patriotic symbols. Assign a symbol to each child (more than one student may be assigned the same symbol). Direct her to draw and cut out a likeness of the symbol on a large sheet of construction paper. Next have her write a paragraph about the symbol, then tape it to the bottom of her symbol. Display the completed projects on a bulletin board. Invite other classes to take a tour of the museum. Then conclude each tour by reciting the Pledge of Allegiance.

- Add an element of high fashion to your classroom by having students design patriotic T-shirts. Distribute a sheet of white construction paper to each student. Instruct him to sketch the outline of a shirt on it before creating a design to inspire patriotism. Encourage students to use patriotic symbols, words, and colors. Then have him cut out his T-shirt. Allow time for a "fashion show" in which students share their creations. Then use the drawings to create a bulletin board titled "We're Patriotic To A T!"

A Treasure Of Maps And Globes

Yo-ho-ho! This treasure of an idea will help students discover the likenesses and differences between maps and globes.

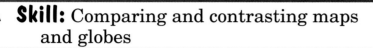

Skill: Comparing and contrasting maps and globes

Estimated Lesson Time: 45 minutes

Teacher Preparation:
1. Duplicate page 37 for each student.
2. Copy each map and globe fact listed below onto a different yellow construction-paper circle (to represent a coin).
3. Place the coins into an empty box.

Materials:
1 copy of page 37 per student
11 labeled yellow construction-paper circles
1 United States map
1 globe
1 empty box (to be used as a treasure box)
tape
scissors
crayons
glue

Background Information:
- *Cartographers* are people who make and study maps.
- *Maps* and *globes* help us find things and places in our world.

Maps	Globes	Both
are flat	are round	have a compass rose, a key or legend, and a scale
are flattened, stretched-out pictures of the earth	show mostly oceans and land	
show many different kinds of places	show the entire earth	become out-of-date (because of new things being built or name and boundary changes)
are drawings or pictures of the earth	show the true shape of the earth	
	are models of the earth	

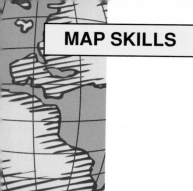

Introducing The Lesson:

Explain to students that long ago pirates traveled the seven seas, hiding their treasures. Show students the construction-paper coins, explaining that they are from a pirate's treasure chest. Ask your students to brainstorm how pirates would have found the treasure they had hidden. Then inform them that many people, including pirates, used maps or globes to find places or things.

Steps:

1. Show students a map and a globe. Have them tell some things they know about each one. List their responses on the chalkboard. Then share the Background Information on page 35.

2. Display the treasure box that contains the construction-paper coins. Draw a large Venn diagram on the board. Label the diagram as shown below. Then invite a volunteer to select a coin from the box. Direct him to read aloud the fact on the coin. Then challenge him to tape the coin to the appropriate place on the diagram. Repeat the process with additional volunteers. When every coin has been placed on the diagram, discuss how maps and globes are the same and different. Remove the coins from the board before beginning Step 3.

3. Distribute one copy of page 37 to each student. Discuss the directions with the students. Then have youngsters complete the page independently.

4. Challenge students to complete the Bonus Box activity.

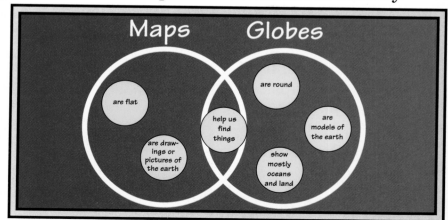

Name_____

A Treasure Of Maps And Globes

Read each fact on the coins below.
If the fact is about a **map,** color it **gray.**
If the fact is about a **globe,** color it **yellow.**
Then cut out each coin and glue it to the
    correct treasure chest.

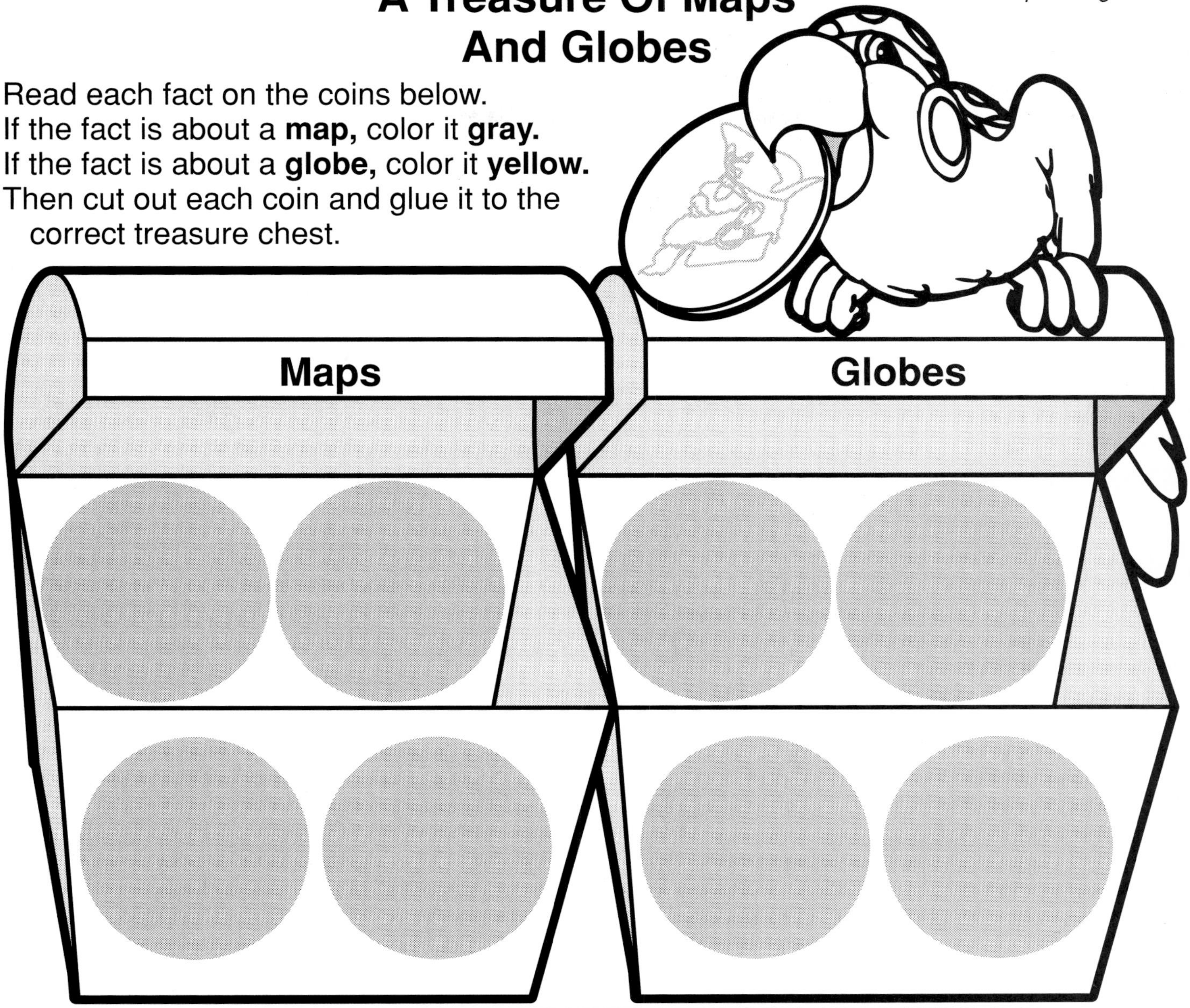

Maps

Globes

Bonus Box: On the back of this paper, write a story about a pirate looking for his lost treasure. Include at least five facts about maps and globes in your story.

©1999 The Education Center, Inc. • *Lifesaver Lessons®* • TEC514

are flat

are models of the earth

show mostly land and oceans

stretch the shape of the earth

show the true shape of the earth

show different kinds of places

are round

are drawings of places

37

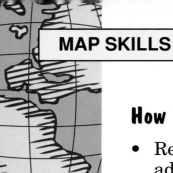
How To Extend The Lesson:

- Reinforce map and globe skills with this treasure hunt game. In advance, label your classroom "North," "South," "East," and "West." To play the game, select a student to be the "pirate." Send the pirate out of the room, or blindfold her so that she cannot see. Next choose another child to hide an object, or "treasure," somewhere in the classroom. Challenge the students to give the pirate cardinal directions to the place where the treasure is hidden. When the pirate finds the treasure, have her pick a new student to search for hidden treasure.

- Share these treasured books about maps and globes!
  –*Me On The Map* by Joan Sweeney (Crown Publishers, 1996)
  –*Maps And Globes* by Jack Knowlton (HarperTrophy®, 1986)
  –*As The Crow Flies: A First Book Of Maps* by Gail Hartman (Aladdin Paperbacks, 1993)
  –*Around The World* by Gary Hincks (Rand McNally & Company, 1997)
  –*Chester The Worldly Pig* by Bill Peet (Houghton Mifflin Company, 1980)

- Share the story *Flat Stanley* by Jeff Brown (HarperTrophy®, 1996). Flat Stanley is a young boy who has the misfortune of having a bulletin board fall on him, making him flat. He is sent in a letter all over the world, having many experiences during his travels. Have your students locate the places Flat Stanley visits on a world map or globe. Next divide students into small groups. Challenge each group to select a new place for Flat Stanley to visit. Then direct each group to collaboratively write a story to describe Flat Stanley's new adventure. Next instruct each group to cut a large rectangle from a large paper grocery bag or a large piece of brown bulletin-board paper. Then instruct each group to color the rectangle to look like a map of where Flat Stanley's new adventure takes place. To make its map look more authentic, have each group fold and then unfold it. Then direct each group to tape its story to the bottom of its map. If desired, collect the stories and staple them to a bulletin board titled "Flat Stanley, World Traveler."

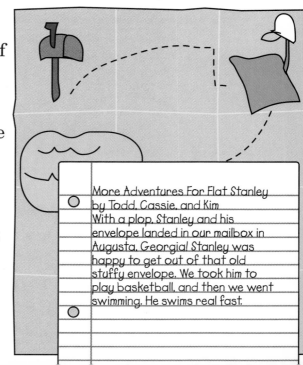

More Adventures For Flat Stanley
by Todd, Cassie, and Kim
With a plop, Stanley and his
envelope landed in our mailbox in
Augusta, Georgia! Stanley was
happy to get out of that old
stuffy envelope. We took him to
play basketball, and then we went
swimming. He swims real fast.

North, South, East, And West!

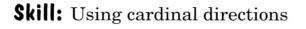

*Keep your students headed in the right direction
with this review of cardinal directions!*

Skill: Using cardinal directions

Estimated Lesson Time: 30 minutes

Teacher Preparation:
1. Duplicate page 41 for each student.
2. Label each of four sheets of construction paper with a different cardinal direction: "N" for north, "S" for south, "E" for east, and "W" for west.

Materials:
1 copy of page 41 per student
labeled cardinal direction signs

Background Information:
- A *compass rose* tells you directions, or which way to go.

- The compass rose was so named because, on paper, the drawing looked something like the petals of a rose.

- Each of the four main arrows on the compass rose points to a different direction. These directions are *north, south, east* and *west.*

- The "N" on the compass rose means *north,* the "S" means *south,* the "E" means *east,* and the "W" means *west.*

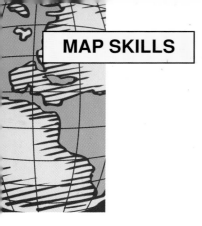
Introducing The Lesson:

Begin the lesson by posting each prepared cardinal direction sign on the appropriate wall of the classroom. Then ask a student volunteer to stand in the middle of the room. Have him follow simple directions, such as "Walk two steps north. Now turn and walk one step east."

Steps:

1. Share the background information on page 39. Tell students that they will be playing a game of I Spy using cardinal directions as clues.

2. Select a volunteer to be the Spy. Instruct the student to secretly think of one object in the room.

3. Direct the Spy to announce, "I spy an object by the [north, south, east, west] wall." Then have him call on another student to identify the object. If the student guesses correctly, he becomes the next Spy. If the student's guess is incorrect, the Spy must give other clues until the object is identified.

4. Play several rounds of I Spy until students exhibit an understanding of using cardinal directions.

5. Distribute a copy of page 41 to each student.

6. Review the directions with the class. Complete the first problem with students; then have youngsters complete the rest of the problems independently.

Which way to go?

North, South, East, And West!

Help Mr. Cardinal find the objects on the map.
Follow the clues to find the object.
Draw the object you land on in the box.

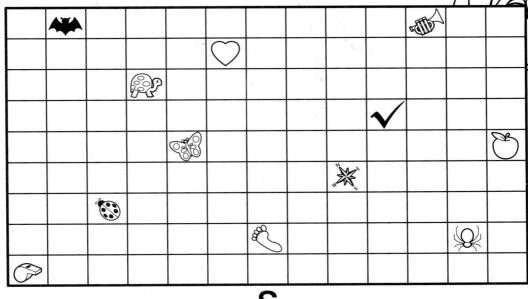

1. Start at the butterfly.
Go east 2 boxes.
Then go south 3 boxes.
Draw a picture of the object you landed on.

5. Start at the footprint.
Go east 4 boxes and north 3 boxes.
Then go west 5 boxes and north 3 boxes.
Draw a picture of the object you landed on.

2. Start at the turtle.
Go north 2 boxes.
Then go west 2 boxes.
Draw a picture of the object you landed on.

6. Start at the compass rose.
Go south 1 box and west 5 boxes.
Then go south 2 boxes and west 3 boxes.
Draw a picture of the object you landed on.

3. Start at the whistle.
Go north 5 boxes.
Then go east 3 boxes and north 1 box.
Draw a picture of the object you landed on.

7. Start at the turtle.
Go east 2 boxes and south 4 boxes.
Then go east 7 boxes and north 2 boxes.
Draw a picture of the object you landed on.

4. Start at the spider.
Go west 4 boxes.
Then go north 4 boxes and east 2 boxes.
Draw a picture of the object you landed on.

8. Start at the heart.
Go south 5 boxes.
Then go west 3 boxes.
Draw a picture of the object you landed on.

How To Extend The Lesson:

- Reinforce the positions on the compass rose with this catchy phrase. Write the phrase "**N**ever **E**at **S**oggy **W**heat" on the chalkboard. Explain to the students that the first letter of each word corresponds with one of the cardinal directions. Challenge students to create their own phrases that reinforce the cardinal directions.

- Use a map to review cardinal directions and map skills. Display a large map of the United States. Challenge students to locate different places on the map. Provide clues such as "This state is north of Kansas." If desired, have student volunteers take turns giving clues about state locations to their classmates.

- Challenge students to write their own cardinal directions. Make a reproducible by using the pattern of the compass rose shown at left and a grid similar to the one on page 41. Include two different pictures in two different boxes. Distribute a copy of the reproducible to each student. Next direct each student to write a set of cardinal directions that starts with one picture and ends at the other. Instruct students to exchange papers. Have each child use her compass rose and a pencil to help her follow the directions. Then have students return the paper to its original owner for checking.

Never Eat Soggy Wheat!

Start at the heart.

Go 2 boxes west.

Go 10 boxes north

and then 5 boxes east....

Pattern

N
W   E
S

©1999 The Education Center, Inc. • Lifesaver Lessons® • TEC514

Welcome To The Neighborhood!

Get to know the neighborhood with the use of a map key.

Skill: Using a map key

Estimated Lesson Time: 30 minutes

Teacher Preparation:
1. Duplicate page 45 for each student.
2. Draw a simple map on a sheet of poster board. (See the example on page 44.)

Materials:
1 copy of page 45 for each student
simple poster board map

Background Information:
A *map* is a special drawing of a place or area.
A *symbol* is a picture that represents an object.
A *map key* explains what each symbol found on the map means.
A *compass rose* is a symbol that shows direction on a map.

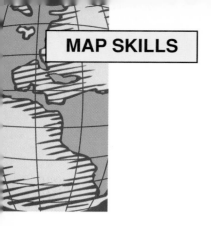

Introducing The Lesson:

Begin the lesson by drawing a simple house shape on the chalkboard. Ask students if they can identify the object you have drawn. Then draw a simple tree shape and repeat the question.

Steps:

1. Explain that the shapes you have drawn are *symbols,* or pictures that represent objects. Tell students that you will show them symbols, like the ones you have drawn, on a map. The symbols on the map will be explained in a map key.

2. Display the prepared map in a prominent location. Ask students to refer to the map key as they answer questions such as
   —How many houses are on the map?
   —How many trees are on the map?
   —What is near the lake?

3. Next explain the use of a compass rose. Review cardinal directions by asking questions such as
   —Is there a house south or north of the lake?
   —What is east of the lake?
   —Are there more houses in the east or in the west?

4. Distribute a copy of page 45 to each student. Review the directions and have each child complete the page independently.

5. Challenge students to complete the Bonus Box activity.

MAP KEY

House

Lake

N
W E
S

Tree

Welcome To The Neighborhood!

Answer the questions.
Use the map key to help you.

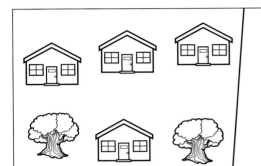
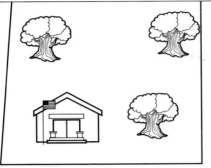
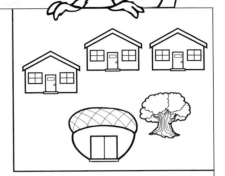

Acorn Avenue

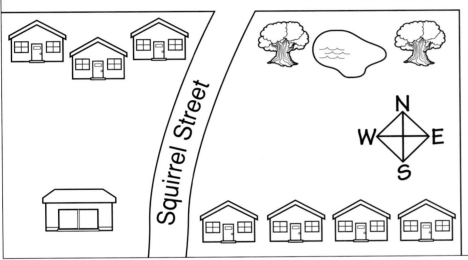

Squirrel Street

Nutty Drive

Map Key
- Rodent School
- house
- tree
- Squirrel Mart
- Nuts R Us
- Acorn Lake

1. How many houses are on the map? _____

2. How many trees are on the map? _____

3. How many trees are north of Acorn Avenue? _____

4. How many houses are west of Squirrel Street? _____

5. Is Rodent School north or south of Acorn Lake? _____

6. How many houses are south of Squirrel Mart? _____

7. What is the name of the store on the east side? _____

Bonus Box: Add an airport to the map. Add an airport symbol to the map key.

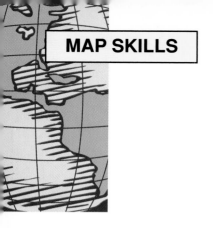
How To Extend The Lesson:

- Have students create a floor map of the area surrounding their school. Take students on a walk around the school. When you return to the room, have the class name the landmarks seen on the walk. With the students' help, use masking tape to map out the area on the carpet or floor in the classroom. Invite small groups of students to design a map key and symbols for the map.

- For an added challenge to the activity described above, have each student write a question that can be answered by looking at the map. Collect the questions. Review map skills by challenging students to answer the questions you read aloud.

- Invite your youngsters to compare the map keys of different maps. Ask each student to bring a map to school. When all the maps have been collected, have students discuss the similarities and differences among the map keys. Then challenge each student to design another symbol for his map key.

- Have each student design a map and map key for a park. Instruct her to include at least five symbols in her map key. For added fun, pair students; then have each pair swap maps. Challenge each youngster to ask her partner questions that can be answered by using the map key.

Map Key

swings
lake
tree
sidewalk
seesaw

PARK

Land Ho!

*Set your youngsters afloat with this booklet-making activity
that reviews geography terms!*

Skill: Identifying geography terms

Estimated Lesson Time: 30 minutes

Teacher Preparation:
1. Duplicate one copy of page 49 for each student.
2. For every two students, program one
   index card with an outdoor activity.
   (See the listed suggestions.)

Materials:
1 copy of page 49 per student
programmed index cards
crayons
scissors
glue

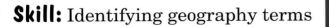

✓ skiing   hiking
✓ skating   canoeing
sledding   walking
✓ swimming   gardening
fishing   biking
✓ running   camping
boating

Background Information:

hill—a raised area of land that is lower than a mountain

lake—a body of water surrounded by land

mountain—a very high piece of land with steep sides

plain—a large, flat area of land

river—a large stream of freshwater that flows into a larger body of water

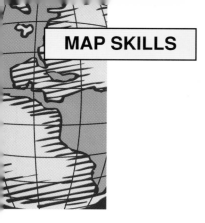

Introducing The Lesson:

Explain to students that they will be pantomiming some outdoor activities. Pair students; then distribute one programmed index card to each pair. Challenge each pair to act out the activity stated on its card. Encourage youngsters to guess the pantomimed activity. Write the name of each activity on the chalkboard as it is correctly identified.

Steps:

1. Share the Background Information on page 47. Ask students to decide where each activity listed on the sign could take place. Lead youngsters to the conclusion that some of the activities could take place on *landforms*—such as hills, islands, mountains, and plains—or in *bodies of water,* such as lakes or rivers.

2. Next distribute one copy of page 49 to each student.

3. Read aloud the title and have the student write his name on the provided line.

4. Then read aloud the definition on booklet page 1. Direct each student to illustrate the hill. Then challenge him to read and illustrate the definition on each remaining page.

5. To complete the booklet, have each student cut apart his pages along the bold lines. Direct him to glue the pages together where indicated. Then, starting with the title page, have him accordion-fold his pages along the dotted lines.

6. Invite students to take their booklets home to share with family members.

Glue page 3 here.

lake—a body of water surrounded by land

2

river—a large stream of fresh-water that flows into a larger body of water

5

hill—a raised area of land that is lower than a mountain

1

plain—a large, flat area of land

4

©1999 The Education Center, Inc.

Land Ho!

And water, too!

Name _____

©1999 The Education Center, Inc.

mountain—a very high piece of land with steep sides

3

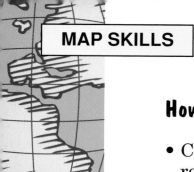

How To Extend The Lesson:

• Challenge your students to work creatively as they design a class-room country that includes landforms and bodies of water. Place a large, sturdy piece of cardboard and a supply of modeling clay in a learning center. Invite each student to visit the center to construct and label a landform or body of water out of the clay. Have him place his creation on the cardboard. Once every student has visited the center, invite the class to vote on a name for the country. Then place the completed project in a prominent location for all to enjoy.

• Impress your students with the geographical record holders listed below. Prompt a class discussion after sharing the information. Challenge students to find each location on a world map. Next have small groups of students illustrate a different record holder on a large sheet of construction paper. Then compile the completed pages into a class booklet titled "Record-Holding Wonders!"

  • Largest Sea—Coral Sea (1,850,200 square miles)
  • Largest Island—Greenland (840,004 square miles)
  • Largest Desert—Sahara in North Africa (3,320,000 square miles)
  • Highest Mountain—Mount Everest in China-Nepal (8,850 miles)
  • Highest Waterfall—Angel Falls in Venezuela (807 miles)
  • Deepest Cave—Jean Bernard in France (1,494 miles)
  • Longest River—Nile in Africa (4,160 miles)
  • Longest Lake—Caspian Sea, north of Iran (143,240 square miles

• Have your students create a wall mural that shows different land-forms and bodies of water. Tape a large piece of bulletin-board paper to a classroom wall. Encourage students to draw and label the different landforms and bodies of water they have learned about. Display the completed mural throughout your study of geography terms.

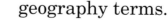

Detecting Diversity

Your young detectives will discover neighborhood similarities and differences with this worldly unit.

Skill: Comparing and contrasting neighborhoods around the world

Estimated Lesson Time: 30 minutes

Teacher Preparation:

1. Duplicate one copy of page 53 for each student.
2. From a discarded magazine, cut out pictures of two children who look distinctly different.

Materials:

1 copy of page 53 per student
2 magazine pictures of children
crayons

Background Information:

- Although neighborhoods around the world can be different, they also have much in common.
- *Comparing* means to identify likenesses. Neighborhoods all around the world have many similarities, such as shelter, places to work and play, and schools.
- *Contrasting* means to identify differences. Climate and natural resources contribute to differences among neighborhoods in different parts of the world. For example, people living in a tropical climate would not live in the same type of shelter as people living in a cold climate.

Introducing The Lesson:

Show students the pictures of the two children. Ask youngsters to tell how these children are alike and how they are different. Then explain that there are many ways people from all over the world are the same and different.

Steps:

1. Prompt a discussion about how neighborhoods are alike and how they are different by sharing the Background Information on page 51.

2. Ask students to consider and discuss the variety of ways people construct their homes in different neighborhoods around the world. Guide students to include several structures and designs in their discussion (see some examples below). Write their responses on the board.

3. Give each student a copy of page 53. Instruct each student to select two different types of shelters and illustrate each one at the top of the page. Then have each student list the likenesses and differences on the appropriate parts of the Venn diagram.

4. To complete the activity, have her choose and write about which of the two homes she prefers.

5. Challenge students to complete the Bonus Box activity.

<u>Sweden</u>
- lumber used for building homes
- wood carved into shapes
- colorful designs painted inside and out

<u>Nova Scotia</u>
- saltbox houses
- shingled exteriors
- steep roofs

<u>Egypt</u>
- bricks made from mud and straw
- thick walls to keep the desert heat out

<u>Ireland</u>
- stone houses with thatched roofs
- thatched roofs made of bundles of straw

<u>Thailand</u>
- houses on poles above water

Name _____

Detecting Diversity

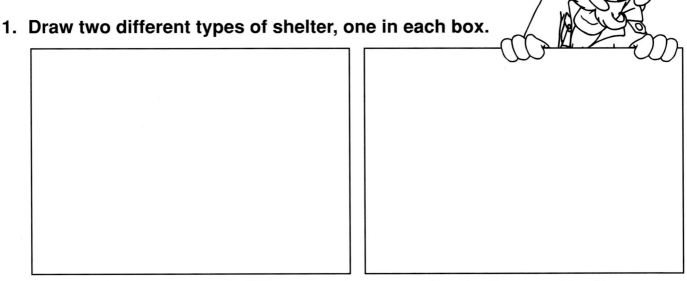

1. **Draw two different types of shelter, one in each box.**

2. **List the likenesses and differences between the shelters on the Venn diagram.**

Differences	**Likenesses**	**Differences**

3. **Choose which home you'd like to live in. On the lines below, write about why you'd prefer living in this home.**

_____

_____

_____

_____

Bonus Box: Imagine you lived on a planet that had trees that grew chocolate bars, rivers that flowed with soda, and mountains that were made of potato chips. On the back of this page, draw a picture of a home you would have on this planet. Write at least three sentences that describe this home.

53

How To Extend The Lesson:

- Challenge students by reading *Houses And Homes* by Ann Morris (Mulberry Books, 1995). Invite students to compare and contrast the homes in the book. After discussing the different homes, divide students into small groups. Instruct each group to create a diorama that showcases a different type of home. Provide each group with an empty shoebox and materials such as construction paper, paint, milk cartons, craft sticks, and clay. Then direct each group to write about its home. When the dioramas are completed, have each group discuss the likenesses and differences between projects.

- Your young detectives will enjoy this puzzling writing activity! Make several copies of the pattern at left to serve as templates. Give each student a 4 1/2" x 12" sheet of light-colored construction paper. To complete the project, each student folds the construction paper in half widthwise. Then he places the roof edge of the template on the fold and traces the house shape. Keeping the paper folded, he cuts out the shape. Next, on the front of his house, he writes a riddle about a type of shelter. He writes the answer on the inside of his house and then decorates the house. Display the riddles on a bulletin board titled "At Home With Riddles!"

- If possible, obtain several *National Geographic* magazines for small groups of students to examine. Challenge each group to search its magazine for a photograph of a neighborhood from somewhere else in the world. Then, on a piece of paper, have each group list the likenesses and differences found between their community and the one in the photograph. Provide time for students to share their findings with the class.

House Pattern

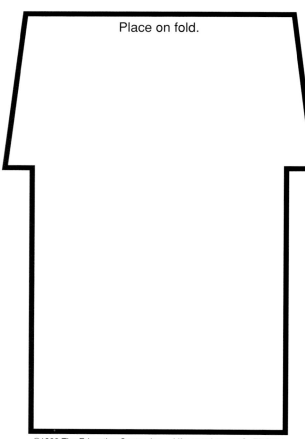

Place on fold.

©1999 The Education Center, Inc. • *Lifesaver Lessons*® • TEC514

Finished Sample

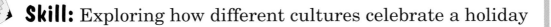

Let's Celebrate!

Take your students on a trip around the world to learn the many ways a special holiday is celebrated.

Skill: Exploring how different cultures celebrate a holiday

Estimated Lesson Time: 45 minutes

Teacher Preparation:
Duplicate page 57 and the cutouts on page 58 for each student.

Materials:
1 copy of page 57 per student
1 set of cutouts per student
large world map
scissors
glue
crayons

Background Information:
Multicultural New Year's Celebrations

Country	Custom
Ecuador	Each family decorates a scarecrow on December 31. Someone writes a will (which lists each family member's faults); then the will is read at midnight. Afterward, the scarecrow and the will are burned in celebration of the new year.
Iran	The 13-day celebration begins on March 20. On the last day, families go on picnics.
Puerto Rico	At midnight on December 31, children throw pails of water out their windows. The water washes bad spirits from the house.
Greece	Children leave their shoes by the fire on December 31. They welcome the new year as they open presents left in the shoes.
China	The new year begins with the second new moon after the winter solstice (between January 17 and February 19) and is celebrated by having a dragon parade.
Vietnam	The new year begins between January 21 and February 19. Tradition includes setting a live carp (a kind of fish) free in a river or pond.

Introducing The Lesson:

Begin the lesson by greeting students with a hearty "Happy New Year!" Explain that although it isn't actually the day we usually celebrate this holiday, you are going to take the class on an imaginary trip around the world to see how different countries bring in the new year.

Steps:

1. Point to the United States on the world map. Tell students that in our country, it is a custom to blow noisemakers at the stroke of midnight to welcome the new year on January 1. Some people also make resolutions or set goals to reach during the upcoming year.

2. Explain to students that some countries celebrate the new year in different ways. Share the Background Information on page 55. Point out each location on the map and describe the New Year's customs of each country.

3. Distribute a copy of page 57 and a set of the cutouts (page 58) to each student. Explain that each youngster is going to make a booklet about the countries and customs that you have just described.

4. Have each student read about the custom described on each booklet page. Direct her to color the pictures on the strip and cut them out. Then instruct her to glue the matching cutout in the box above each custom.

5. Have each student cut out the booklet strips along the bold lines. Have her lay the two strips end-to-end and glue them together to make one long strip.

6. Direct students to accordion-fold their booklets along the thin lines as shown.

7. Have students take their booklets home to share with family members.

In Ecuador, the family decorates a scarecrow. They burn it at midnight on December 31.

(3)

The End

In Puerto Rico, children throw pails of water out thier windows on December 31. The water washes bad spirits from the house.

(2)

In Vietnam, the new year is celebrated in January or Febuary. People set live carp (a kind of fish) free in ponds and rivers.

(6)

In China, the new year starts in January or February. There is a dragon parade with lots of fireworks.

(1)

In Greece, children find presents inside thier shoes on January 1. They start the new year as they open the presents.

(5)

Let's Celebrate!

Name

In Iran, the new year begins on March 20. After celebrating for 13 days, families go on picnics.

(4)

Glue page 3 here.

How To Extend The Lesson:

• With the help of parent volunteers, hold an international celebration to increase students' awareness of other cultures. Include some of the following activities.

—Invite students to wear ethnic costumes such as Mexican sombreros and serapes, African dashikis, Japanese kimonos, Indian saris, and Native American moccasins.

—Teach students how to count or say key phrases in a variety of languages.

—Plan an international feast featuring a variety of foods for students to sample, such as Mexican enchiladas, Jewish bagels with cream cheese and lox, Italian pasta, Japanese tea, German sausage, African rice, and Chinese fortune cookies.

—Conclude the celebration of cultures with games, music, stories, and dances significant to different ethnic groups.

—After the celebration, have each student draw a picture to show her favorite part of the international celebration. Use the completed drawing to make a bulletin board or "culture collage" highlighting the unique and special qualities of each ethnic group.

Patterns
Use with Steps 3 and 4 on page 56.

Exploring how from different cultures celebrate a holiday

Timely Timelines

Students will find arranging holidays in chronological order a breeze with these timely timeline activities!

Skill: Identifying and sequencing major U.S. holidays using timelines

Estimated Lesson Time: 30 minutes

Teacher Preparation:
Duplicate page 61 for each student.

Materials:
1 copy of page 61 per student
1 sheet of chart paper
1 calendar (for teacher use)

Background Information:
A timeline can show a long period of time. It can keep track of a year or more. Reading timelines can help you understand the order of important events in history. You read a timeline from left to right, like a sentence. The earliest events are on the left. The events that happened later are on the right.

Introducing The Lesson:

Begin by inviting students to raise their hands if they like parties. Then display a calendar and begin thumbing through it. Ask the class to name possible times throughout the year you could have a holiday party or get-together. List their responses on a sheet of chart paper in random order.

Steps:

1. Discuss the date of each holiday and write it on the chart. Discuss how some holidays (such as Thanksgiving) do not have a specific date.

2. After the class has developed a sufficient list of holidays and dates, challenge youngsters to discuss whether the holidays on the list are in the correct order. Explain that timelines help keep track of dates. Then share the Background Information on page 59.

3. Next draw a horizontal timeline on the chalkboard and label it at monthly increments (from January to December) as shown.

4. Refer to the student-generated list of holidays. Enlist students' help in determining a symbol for each holiday, to make it easier to mark the holidays on the timeline. (For example, use a party hat for New Year's Day and a heart for Valentine's Day.) Announce a holiday and have a student mark the timeline on the chalkboard with the appropriate symbol. Continue in this manner until all the holidays have been marked on the timeline.

5. Distribute a copy of page 61 to each student. Read the directions together and have each student complete the page independently.

6. Challenge students to complete the Bonus Box activity.

Identifying and sequencing major U.S. holidays using timelines

Name _____

Timely Timelines

Use the Holiday Date Bank to write the dates on each holiday shape.
Then write the letter for each holiday on the timeline above the correct month.

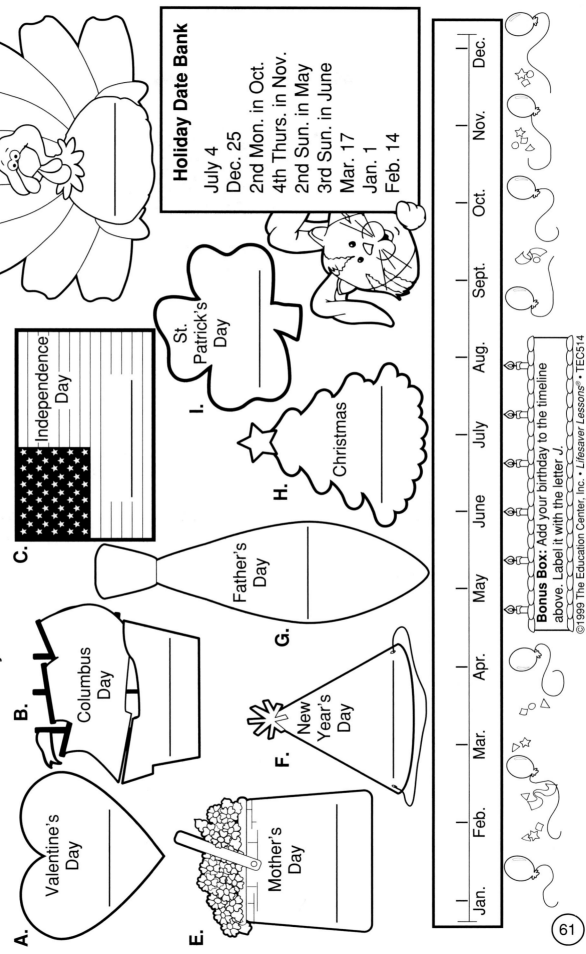

Holiday Date Bank

July 4
Dec. 25
2nd Mon. in Oct.
4th Thurs. in Nov.
2nd Sun. in May
3rd Sun. in June
Mar. 17
Jan. 1
Feb. 14

A. Valentine's Day _____

B. Columbus Day _____

C. Independence Day _____

D. Thanksgiving _____

E. Mother's Day _____

F. New Year's Day _____

G. Father's Day _____

H. Christmas _____

I. St. Patrick's Day _____

Jan. | Feb. | Mar. | Apr. | May | June | July | Aug. | Sept. | Oct. | Nov. | Dec.

Bonus Box: Add your birthday to the timeline above. Label it with the letter *J.*

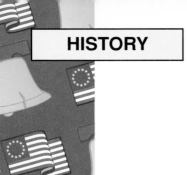

How To Extend The Lesson:

- Enlist your students' help in making a human timeline. In advance, apply a long strip of masking tape to the floor of your classroom or along a wall in the hallway. Label colored index cards with each month and tape them in order along the masking-tape timeline. Then write several holidays on individual index cards. Give each child a card. Have students sequence themselves in order along the timeline. If desired, repeat the activity using students' birthdays.

- Go beyond the average American holiday. Obtain a copy of a holiday book that contains some unusual celebrations. *The Holiday Handbook* by Carol Barkin (Clarion Books, 1994) is one such book. Arranged by seasons, this delightful book centers on unusual holidays and celebrations. After sharing some parts of the book, invite students to make timelines to include some of the unusual ones listed.

- Have each child select a holiday celebrated in the United States. Invite him to write an acrostic poem of his chosen holiday. To do this, a student writes the name of his holiday down the left side of a sheet of paper. Next he uses each letter in the name for the initial letter of a word or phrase that describes the holiday. Once students have shared their poems with their classmates, display the poems timeline-fashion on a wall for all to enjoy.

H aunted
A ll kids dress up
L ittle pumpkins
L ots of treats
O wls hoot
W itches fly
E veryone is happy
E ating candy
N ighttime

Transportation Of Yesterday And Today

*Whether it's by land, sea, or air, the way we get from
here to there has changed throughout the years.*

Skill: Comparing and contrasting transportation of today
with that of the past

Estimated Lesson Time: 30 minutes

Teacher Preparation:
1. Duplicate page 65 for each student.
2. Write the Background Information shown below on a sheet of
   chart paper.
3. Draw a large Venn diagram on the chalkboard. Label the left side
   "Long Ago," the middle "Both," and the right side "Today." Then
   write the title "Transportation" at the top.

Materials:
1 copy of page 65 for each student
chart paper with Background Information
labeled Venn diagram
markers
car keys

Background Information:
    There are three main types of transportation: land, air, and water. Land
vehicles, such as cars, need roads. Air transportation, such as airplanes, needs
airports. Water transportation, such as ships, requires docks and ports.
    Long ago, the main purpose of vehicles was to transport people and goods.
For most of history, however, transportation was very slow. Before steam-pow-
ered vehicles, many people relied on wind or muscle power to move them.
Animal-drawn wagons or carriages traveled over dirt roads. Mules or horses
walked alongside canals and rivers pulling boats by ropes.
    Today's vehicles help us travel and transport goods all over the world. They
are faster and more dependable. People now use transportation for fun, work,
and travel. Unfortunately most forms of today's transportation cause air
pollution, traffic, and high fuel use.

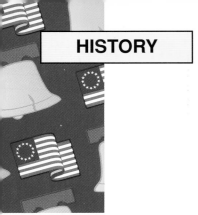

Introducing The Lesson:

Grab your students' attention by jangling your car keys loudly in the front of the room. Then ask students to name how they came to school today. Provide time for students to share their responses.

Steps:

1. Ask students to name all the examples of transportation they know. As each student gives an example, have her determine if it was used long ago, today, or both long ago and today. Then write the example in the appropriate section of the Venn diagram. (See the diagram below.)

2. Discuss the resulting Venn diagram with the class. Next display the Background Information. Then have a volunteer read it aloud. Encourage students to discuss the differences between the vehicles of today with those of long ago.

3. Distribute a copy of page 65 to each student. Read the directions together and then have each student complete her page independently.

4. Challenge students to complete the Bonus Box activity.

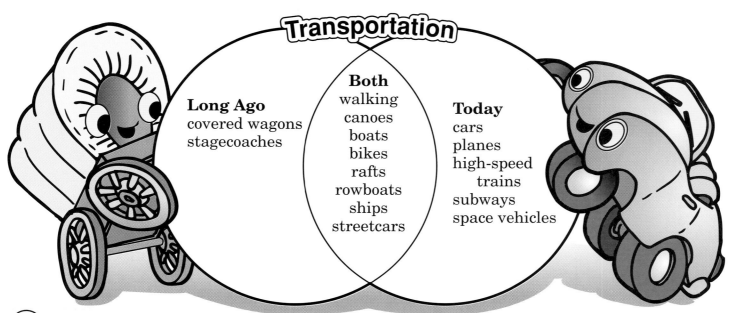

Transportation

Long Ago
covered wagons
stagecoaches

Both
walking
canoes
boats
bikes
rafts
rowboats
ships
streetcars

Today
cars
planes
high-speed
    trains
subways
space vehicles

Name_____

Transportation
Of Yesterday And Today

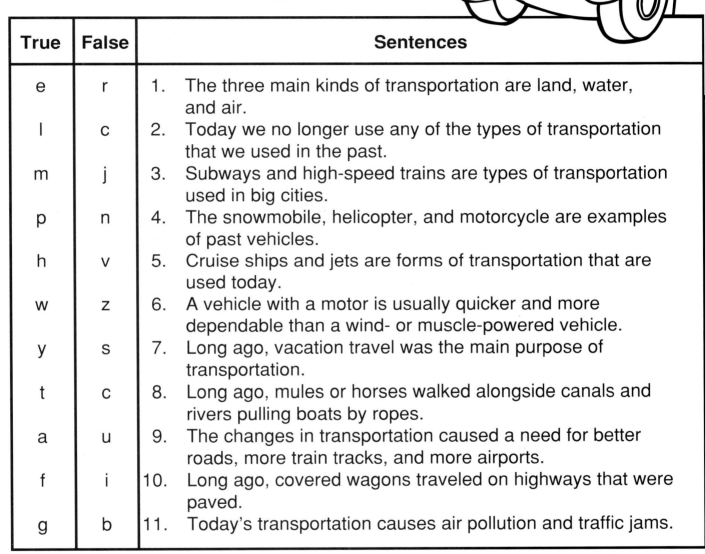

Read each sentence.
Decide if the sentence is true or false.
Circle the letter in the matching column.

True	False	Sentences
e	r	1. The three main kinds of transportation are land, water, and air.
l	c	2. Today we no longer use any of the types of transportation that we used in the past.
m	j	3. Subways and high-speed trains are types of transportation used in big cities.
p	n	4. The snowmobile, helicopter, and motorcycle are examples of past vehicles.
h	v	5. Cruise ships and jets are forms of transportation that are used today.
w	z	6. A vehicle with a motor is usually quicker and more dependable than a wind- or muscle-powered vehicle.
y	s	7. Long ago, vacation travel was the main purpose of transportation.
t	c	8. Long ago, mules or horses walked alongside canals and rivers pulling boats by ropes.
a	u	9. The changes in transportation caused a need for better roads, more train tracks, and more airports.
f	i	10. Long ago, covered wagons traveled on highways that were paved.
g	b	11. Today's transportation causes air pollution and traffic jams.

Solve the riddle below.
For each number, write the circled letter.

What has a motor and a foot, and runs but goes nowhere?

___ ___ ___ ___ ___ ___ ___ ___ ___ ___ ___ ___ ___ ___ ___ ___ ___ !
10 8   10 7   9   7 1 6 10 4 11   3 9 2 5 10 4 1

Bonus Box: On the back of this paper, draw your favorite type of transportation. Write at least two sentences that tell why it is your favorite.

65

How To Extend The Lesson:

- Challenge your students to design a stamp series for transportation. Give each child a 9" x 9" piece of white construction paper. (If desired, scallop the edges of the squares to resemble stamps.) Divide the class into two groups. Have one group illustrate vehicles of today on its squares and the other group draw vehicles of the past. Display the completed stamps in your classroom for a "stamp-errific" display.

- Have each student write a journal entry about how he might get to school if he lived in another part of the world. Share the story *This Is The Way We Go To School: A Book About Children Around The World* by Edith Baer (Scholastic Inc., 1992). Then have each child choose a way he could get to school that is different than his usual one. Instruct each student to write a journal entry describing his experience. Provide time for students to share their entries with their classmates.

- Challenge students to make an ABC book of transportation. Assign each child a different letter of the alphabet. Instruct the student to write her assigned letter in the top right corner of a sheet of construction paper. Next have the student write the name of a type of transportation (from the past or present) that begins with her assigned letter. Then have her illustrate her type of transportation. Sequence the completed pages in alphabetical order before binding them into a class booklet. Then place the booklet at your reading center for all to enjoy!

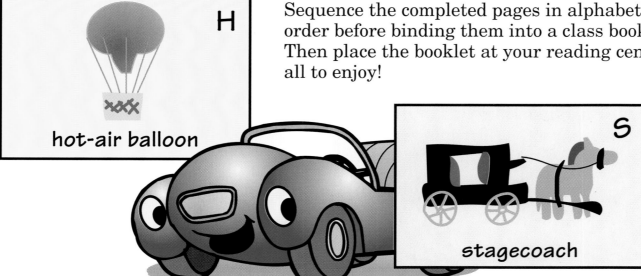

H
hot-air balloon

S
stagecoach

Thank You, Mr. President!

Take a look at the many accomplishments these historical figures have made for our country!

Skill: Identifying contributions of significant historical figures

Estimated Lesson Time: 30 minutes

Teacher Preparation:
1. Duplicate page 69 for each student.
2. Gather the materials listed below.

Materials:
1 copy of page 69 per student
1 brad per student
scissors

Background Information:
One of the greatest rights of an American citizen is the right to participate in electing the president of the United States. The Constitution states that we can elect any person with the following qualifications:

• He/she is a natural-born citizen.
• He/she has lived in the United States at least 14 years.
• He/she is at least 35 years old.

In addition, the 22nd amendment limits a president to serving two terms in office.

Introducing The Lesson:

Ask students to imagine that they are participants on a quiz show. The object of the game is to earn a star for each correct answer. Challenge students to earn at least three stars (which you will draw on the chalkboard) as they answer the following questions:

— What do we call the person who acts as leader of our country?
— Who was our first president?
— Who is our current president?
— Where does the president live?

Steps:

1. Congratulate students for their efforts. Then share the Background Information on page 67.

2. Explain that besides leading our country, presidents often make other important contributions to the United States. Then share these examples with students:

    — A president created a program called Social Security, which allows you to get part of your paycheck after you retire.
    — A president created the Peace Corps, an organization that helps bring peace to all parts of the world.
    — A president doubled the size of the United States by buying land from France.

3. Distribute a copy of page 69 to each child. Have a volunteer read aloud one of the sentences in the lower right-hand corner. Have students discuss which president listed on the wheel made the contribution. Repeat until each sentence has been read and discussed.

4. Next instruct each student to cut out the pattern pieces, reread each sentence, and glue it below the appropriate president's name.

5. Have the student attach the smaller wheel to the center of the larger one with a brad. Challenge each youngster to match each picture with its president.

Identifying contributions of significant historical figures

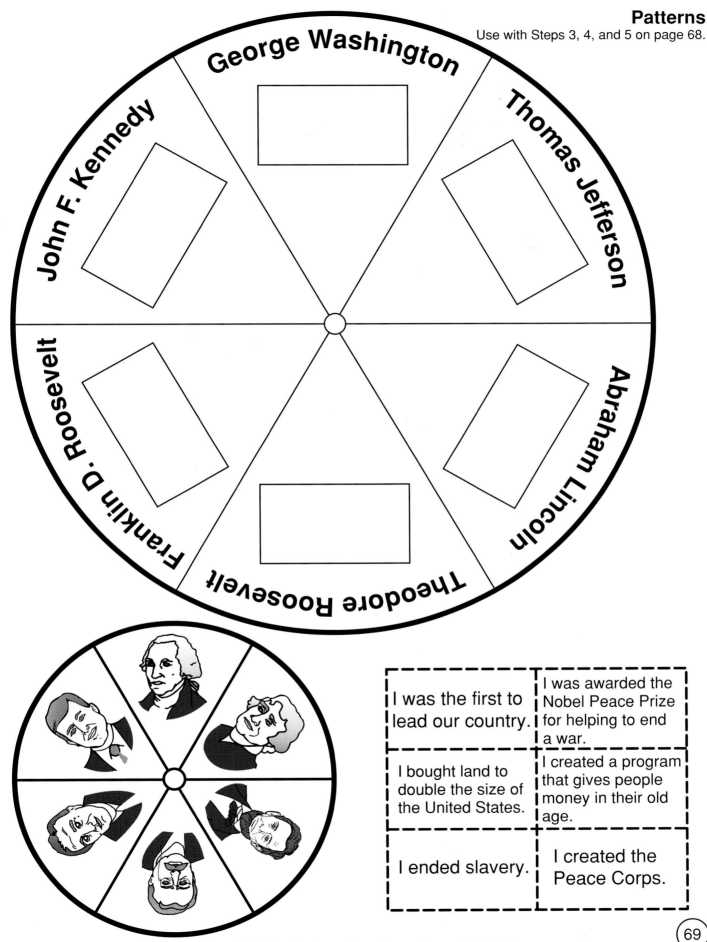

George Washington

John F. Kennedy

Thomas Jefferson

Franklin D. Roosevelt

Abraham Lincoln

Theodore Roosevelt

I was the first to lead our country.	I was awarded the Nobel Peace Prize for helping to end a war.
I bought land to double the size of the United States.	I created a program that gives people money in their old age.
I ended slavery.	I created the Peace Corps.

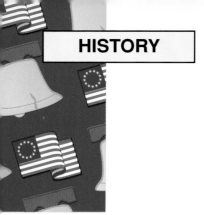
How To Extend The Lesson:

• Challenge each student to interview a family member to find out which president he most admires and why. Provide time for students to discuss their interview results with the class. If desired, extend the activity by having students make a graph to show which presidents were named most often.

• Share these presidential stories with your future voters:

—*The President: America's Leader* by Mary Oates Johnson (Raintree Steck-Vaughn Publishers, 1996)
—*Buttons For General Washington* by Peter and Connie Roop (Carolrhoda Books, Inc.; 1987)
—*Meet Thomas Jefferson* by Marvin Barrett (Random House, Inc.; 1989)
—*Abe Lincoln's Hat* by Martha Brenner (Random House, Inc.; 1994)

• Have each student select a president that has made a significant contribution to the United States. Have her write him a thank-you note for his efforts and hard work. Display the completed notes on a bulletin board titled "Thank You, Mr. President!"

Thank You, Abraham Lincoln!

Dear President Lincoln, I am so glad that you ended slavery. Thank you for making our world a better place!

Your friend,
Caroline

Down To Basics

Help your youngsters understand that what they want is not always what they need!

Skill: Comparing and contrasting wants and needs

Estimated Lesson Time: 25 minutes

Teacher Preparation:
Duplicate page 73 for each student.

Materials:
1 copy of page 73 for each student
1 sheet of drawing paper for each student
glue
crayons
scissors

Background Information:

- **Needs**—things a person must have to live. The three basic needs are *food, clothing,* and *shelter.* People also need love and care.

- **Wants**—things people would like to have but do not need.

- In the past, most people worked with their families to grow or make the things they wanted and needed. They would grow fruits, grain, and vegetables; raise animals; sew clothes; and build their own homes. Today it is easier for most people to buy what they want and need at stores. Much has changed over time, but people's basic needs remain the same.

Introducing The Lesson:

Distribute one sheet of drawing paper to each student. Give each student 3–5 minutes to illustrate as many items in his home as he can. Then have him draw a star beside the three most important items on his paper.

Steps:

1. Share the Background Information on page 71. Explain that a *need* is something you must have to live, and a *want* is something that you would like to have, but do not need. Basic needs include food, shelter, and clothing.

2. Have each student revisit his paper. Direct him to circle all his *needs* with one color crayon; then have him circle all his *wants* in another color.

3. Instruct each youngster to share his paper with a partner. Challenge each student to compare and contrast his wants and needs with his classmate's.

4. Distribute a copy of page 73 to each student. Review the directions together. Then remind students that although each item on the page can be used for camping, Rodney Raccoon may only bring those things which are considered basic needs. Then have students complete the page independently.

5. Challenge students to complete the Bonus Box activity.

Down To Basics

Rodney Raccoon is shopping for his camping trip.
He only has room to pack his basic needs.
Color and cut out each picture.
Glue Rodney's basic needs to the appropriate shopping bags.

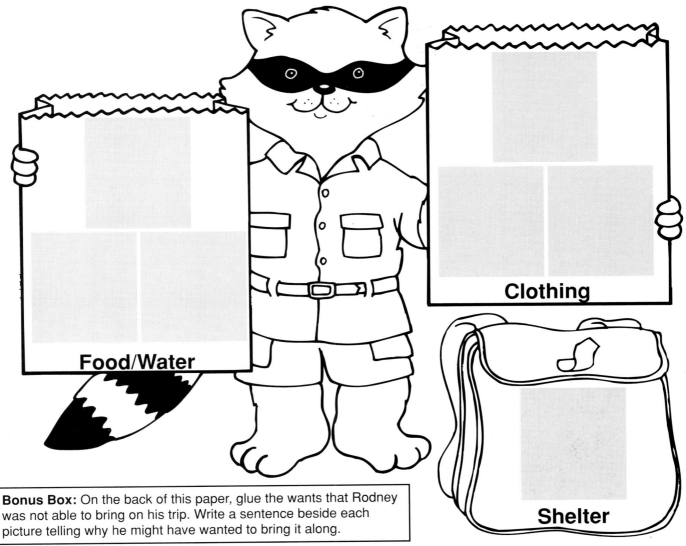

Food/Water

Clothing

Shelter

Bonus Box: On the back of this paper, glue the wants that Rodney was not able to bring on his trip. Write a sentence beside each picture telling why he might have wanted to bring it along.

©1999 The Education Center, Inc. • *Lifesaver Lessons®* • TEC514 • Key p. 95

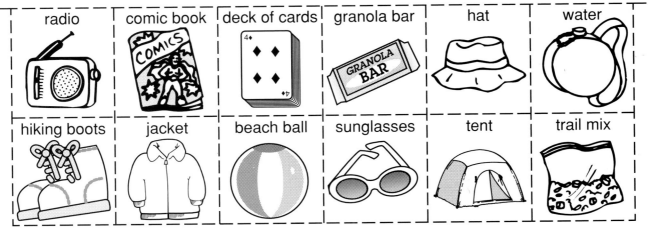

| radio | comic book | deck of cards | granola bar | hat | water |
| hiking boots | jacket | beach ball | sunglasses | tent | trail mix |

How To Extend The Lesson:

- Use this simple activity to ensure that each student in your class can distinguish between wants and needs. Provide each child with an index card. Instruct each student to write the word "Needs" on one side of his card, and "Wants" on the other side. Then call out assorted items—such as apple, video game, apartment, and pencil—one at a time. After each item is named, have students show you the corresponding side of their cards.

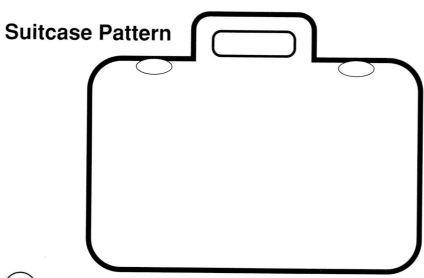

- Ask students to generate a list of things which are not considered the three basic needs, but would be very difficult to live without—like money, transportation, friendship, or medicine. List the students' responses on the chalkboard. Then provide each student with a sheet of story paper. Ask him to choose the item on the board that he most feels should be included among the basic needs. Have him write a paragraph explaining why this need is important; then direct him to illustrate it as desired.

- Reinforce wants and needs with this activity. Enlarge and duplicate one copy of the suitcase pattern below for each student. Direct each student to label one side of his suitcase "Wants" and the other side "Needs." Next have each student think of at least ten items he would like to take with him on an imaginary trip. Challenge him to include a balance of at least five wants and five needs. Then instruct him to list or illustrate each item on the appropriate side of his suitcase. Provide time for youngsters to compare their wants and needs to their classmates'.

Suitcase Pattern

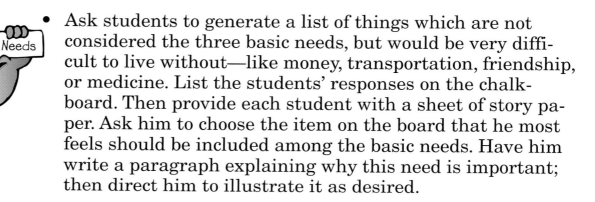

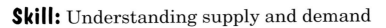

It's In Demand!

Strengthen students' understanding of
supply and demand with this engaging game.

Skill: Understanding supply and demand

Estimated Lesson Time: 30 minutes

Teacher Preparation:
Duplicate page 77 for each student.

Materials:
1 copy of page 77 for each student
1 additional sheet of white paper
  per student
scissors
glue

Background Information:
- **Supply**—the number of items available
- **Demand**—the number of items wanted
- **Scarcity**—the lack of goods or resources as compared to what is wanted

When the *supply* is greater than the *demand,* store owners have too many items on their shelves. Sometimes owners drop prices so that it will be easier to sell the extra items.

When the *demand* is greater than the *supply,* the store owner may not be able to keep enough items in stock. The item becomes worth more because so many people want it, and the price may increase.

Things are considered more valuable when they are *scarce.*

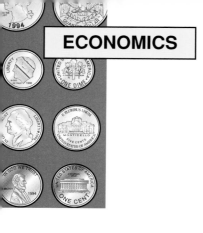

Introducing The Lesson:

Ask students to name items that have been popular and in demand. Reinforce examples such as beanbag toys, video games, newly released rental movies, and certain brands of sneakers. Help students to conclude that when these items are in demand, they can be hard to find and higher in price.

Steps:

1. Share the Background Information on page 75.

2. Distribute a copy of page 77 to each child. Then pair students. Distribute one pair of scissors to each twosome.

3. Ask students what the problem would be if you instructed them all to cut out their game cards. Guide students to understand that there are not enough scissors to go around. Inform students that this is an example of demand that is greater than supply.

4. Distribute additional scissors and instruct students to cut out their game cards. Explain that the cards will be used to play a game about supply and demand.

5. Explain the rules of the game as follows:
   —All players place their cards facedown in the center of their group.
   —Each student in the group takes a turn selecting two cards and placing them faceup. She reads the passages aloud and/or identifies the picture(s). If the cards make a match (a picture matches a passage), she keeps the cards and takes another turn. (Cards are coded for self-checking.) If the cards do not make a match, she returns them to their facedown position, and the next player takes his turn.
   —Play continues until all cards have been matched. The player who has the most cards wins!

6. When the game is over, have each student collect a complete set of cards. Direct him to glue the cards in matching pairs onto another sheet of paper.

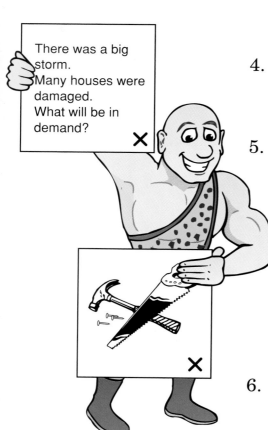

The town is having a picnic.
People will buy food for the picnic.
What will be in demand? ●

The weather is getting colder.
Soon it will snow.
What will be in demand? ■

People are starting to think about spring.
They know that April can be a rainy month.
What will be in demand? ▲

 ●

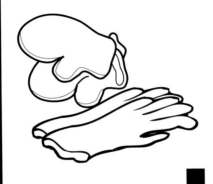 ■

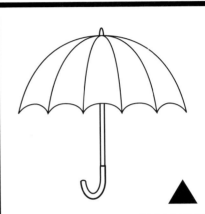 ▲

Something important has happened.
Everyone wants to know more about it.
What will be in demand? ♥

It's time for school to start.
Children will need supplies.
What will be in demand? ★

There was a big storm.
Many houses were damaged.
What will be in demand? ✕

  ♥

 ★

 ✕

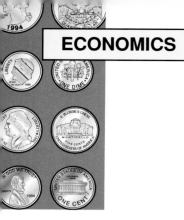

How To Extend The Lesson:

- Ask students to discuss the concept of supply and demand with family members. Have each student bring to school a list of items that family members can recall being limited, and, if possible, the reasons why. Then discuss the completed lists in class.

- Have students think of how natural resources such as air, water, land, plants, and animals could be affected by scarcity. Discuss the importance of protecting the environment and our resources. Then have each student make a poster encouraging others to help take care of our planet.

- Have children consider the fact that the demand for services can exceed the supply. Discuss with your students services that can be affected by factors such as weather, or illness. Then have students role-play situations in which service workers must explain to customers why the services are not readily available.

- Encourage each student to draw a toy that would be in demand. Have her use her marketing skills to write an advertisement for her product, reminding her that her toy must have a special feature to make customers want to buy it. Provide time for each student to "advertise" her toy to the class. Encourage students to discuss what would happen if their products were popular and in demand.

Buy a Fuzzby!

It talks!
It sings!
It eats your broccoli!

Everyone loves Betsy!

The doll who tells you how to dress her.

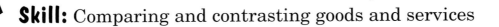

All Around The Town

This activity will teach students that goods and services are provided all around the town.

Skill: Comparing and contrasting goods and services

Estimated Lesson Time: 45 minutes

Teacher Preparation:

1. Duplicate a copy of page 81 for each student.
2. Place an article of clothing, a can or box of food, and a toy in a shopping bag. (Substitute magazine pictures or drawings, if desired.)

Materials:

1 copy of page 81 per student
two 1" x 18" strips of black construction paper per student
one 1" x 12" strip of black construction paper per student
one 12" x 18" piece of green construction paper per student
crayons
scissors
glue
shopping bag filled with items described in "Teacher Preparation"

Background Information:

- **goods**—merchandise that people make or grow

- **service**—work that a person or company provides for others

- In the United States, people are able to own and run businesses without much government control. Each business tries to provide goods or services that are useful and well made. To succeed and compete with other businesses, these goods and services are offered at reasonable prices. This is the free enterprise system, upon which our country's economy is modeled.

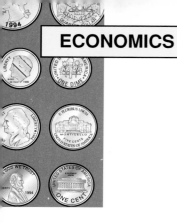

Introducing The Lesson:

Begin the lesson by showing your students the prepared bag. Explain that you went to several shops in town and purchased a variety of goods. Write the word *goods* on the chalkboard.

Steps:

1. Remove one item from the bag. Ask students to guess the type of store in which it was purchased, and record reasonable responses under the word *goods*. Repeat this process for each item in the bag.

2. When the bag is empty, explain that you also spent some money on services, which could not be carried in a bag. Write the word *services* on the chalkboard.

3. Provide students with several scenarios, such as "I had my teeth cleaned," "I had the flat tire on my car repaired," or "I had my clothes cleaned." Ask students to guess where you'd been. Record reasonable responses under the word *services*.

4. Explain that money can be used to buy goods (merchandise) or services (work). Review the Background Information on page 79 with students.

5. Provide each student with the green and black construction paper and glue. Have each student glue the black strips onto his green construction paper as shown. Then direct each child to label one 18-inch strip "Goods Road," the other 18-inch strip "Service Street," and the 9-inch strip "[Student's name] Lane."

6. Distribute a copy of page 81 to each student. Ask each youngster to color and then cut out the buildings. Next have him glue each shop on the appropriate street, indicating whether goods or services are provided there.

7. Then have students exchange papers. Challenge youngsters to discuss why each building is placed in its location.

1ST PROMISE BANK

Bake-A-Cake Bakery

We Make Scents Florist

Cathy's CAR REPAIR

Fancy Fashions CLOTHING STORE

FUN FOR YOU TOY STORE

Bob's BARBER SHOP

SUPER FOOD GROCERY STORE

MILK 2¹⁹ GAL

Special! EGGS 99¢ DOZ

How To Extend The Lesson:

- Extend students' understanding of goods and services with this letter-writing activity. Ask students to think of a good or service they recently received and especially enjoyed or appreciated. (Perhaps a student is thankful for a new board game, a good dental checkup, or a nice haircut.) Have each youngster write a thank-you letter to the person, store, or company that provided the good or service. Encourage students to hand-deliver or send their thank-you notes.

- Explain to students that tax money is used to pay for services from the government. These services can be found in and outside of the local community. Elicit a student-generated list of government services on the board (such as a school, post office, police station, or library). Then provide each child with two 3-inch squares of white paper. Have each youngster draw and color a different community building on each square. Invite each student to cut out the buildings and glue them beside the others on Service Street.

- Tie your study of goods and services to a review of community helpers with this fun guessing game. Divide the class into two teams. Invite a student from the first team to come to the front of the room. Secretly assign her a career from the list shown. Ask the student to give three clues about her occupation to the class. If a member of her team can guess her occupation, the team earns one point. If the team can tell whether she provides a good or service, it earns an additional point. Play continues, alternating between the two teams, until each child has had a turn to give clues. The team with the most points wins!

Workers Who Provide Goods
Florist
Chef
Fisherman
Grocer
Butcher
Miner
Farmer
Photographer
Artist

Workers Who Provide Services
Firefighter
Mail carrier
Custodian
Hairstylist/Barber
Veterinarian
Operator
Lifeguard
Librarian
Crossing guard
Lawyer

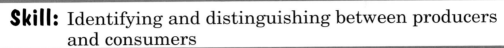

Producing Sharp Consumers

Your young consumers are sure to profit when they complete this lesson on producers and consumers.

Skill: Identifying and distinguishing between producers and consumers

Estimated Lesson Time: 40 minutes

Teacher Preparation:
1. Duplicate page 85 for each student.
2. Duplicate the response triangle pattern on page 86 for each student.
3. Collect several classroom items (such as a calculator, a box of crayons, a book, a box of tissues, a small article of clothing, and a food item) and place them in a shopping bag.

Materials:
1 copy of page 85 for each student
1 copy of the pattern on page 86 for each student
1 shopping bag
several small classroom items

Shop till I drop!

Background Information:
- The United States produces (makes) and consumes (buys) goods and services to meet the wants and needs of its people.

- A *need* is something that is necessary for living. A *want* is something a person would like, but does not need in order to survive.

- *Goods* and *services* are things that can be bought and sold. Goods can be grown or made. Services are provided by people to help the public.

- *Producers* are people who provide goods or services that can be bought and sold. Examples of producers include cooks, farmers, bakers, and factory workers.

- *Consumers* are people who use goods and services. Examples of consumers include parents, moviegoers, video renters, restaurant patrons, students, mall shoppers, and bank customers.

ECONOMICS

Introducing The Lesson:

Display the prepacked shopping bag. Tell the students that you did a little shopping for school today. Unload the bag, one item at a time. Ask students to guess where each item was purchased. On the chalkboard, list students' responses, which may include guesses such as a *factory, store, farm, mall,* or specific store name. Explain that someone sold you each item, and before that, someone made it.

Steps:

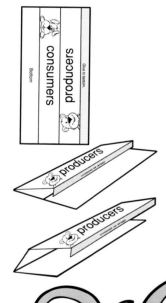

1. Share the Background Information on page 83. Explain to students that when you are shopping, you are a consumer. Encourage the class to brainstorm a list of other consumers and producers.

2. Next inform students that they are going to play a game to show their knowledge of producers and consumers. Distribute a copy of the pattern on page 86 to each student. Instruct each child to cut out the pattern along the dotted lines, fold it along the solid lines, and then glue the two outer flaps together as shown.

3. To play the game, announce a consumer or producer role. (See the Background Information on page 83 for examples.) Instruct each child to decide whether the role described names a producer or a consumer. Then have her display the correct side of the response triangle on her desk, facing you. Discuss the appropriate answer. Continue the activity until students appear confident in their responses.

4. Next give each student a copy of page 85. Review the directions with the class. Provide time for students to complete the activity independently.

5. Challenge students to complete the Bonus Box activity.

Producing Sharp Consumers

Read the information in the box.
Decide which person below is a *producer* and which is a *consumer.*
Use the color code to color the symbol beside each item.
Write the reason for your choice on the blank.

Producers	Consumers
A producer is someone who provides goods or services that can be bought and sold. • The maker	A consumer is a person who buys the goods or services available for sale. • The customer

$$ 1. farmer _____

$$ 2. Mom and Dad _____

$$ 3. TV manufacturer _____

$$ 4. karate teacher _____

$$ 5. sports fan _____

$$ 6. shoe repairman _____

$$ 7. child in toy store _____

$$ 8. traveler _____

Bonus Box: On the back of this paper, list three things you would like to purchase as a *consumer.* For each one, write a sentence that tells what *producer* you would need to visit.

Color Code
green = consumer
purple = producer

85

How To Extend The Lesson:

- Challenge youngsters to work together to create a mural depicting producers and consumers. Divide a large piece of bulletin-board paper into five sections. Label each section with a different heading: "Food," "Housing," "Clothing," "Transportation," and "Miscellaneous." Encourage the class to cut out advertisements from discarded magazines and circulars that fit into each category. Then have students glue their pictures to the appropriate section of the paper. Mount the completed mural and the heading "Second Grade Satisfies Consumers' Wants And Needs!" to a wall outside your classroom.

- Reinforce the concept of distinguishing between producers and consumers with this creative idea. Secretly assign each youngster a different producer or consumer. Then provide each student with a sheet of drawing paper and instruct her to illustrate her person. Then challenge her to show the class her picture and give clues until the identity of her person is guessed. Then collect the papers and display them on a bulletin board titled "Producer Or Consumer?"

Pattern
Use with Steps 2 and 3 on page 84.

Glue to bottom.

producers

 consumers

Bottom

The World Of Work

*Wants and needs, goods and services, buying and saving—
they're all part of the world of work!*

 Skill: Explaining uses of money as a means of exchange

Estimated Lesson Time: 30 minutes

Teacher Preparation:
Duplicate page 89 for each student.

Materials:
1 copy of page 89 per student

Background Information:
Wants are things a person or group wishes to have. *Needs* are things a person or group must have for its survival and well-being. *Goods* are items or products made or grown by people or companies. *Services* are jobs people do to help others. *Income* is the money people earn for the jobs they do. People use their income to buy the goods and services they want and need.

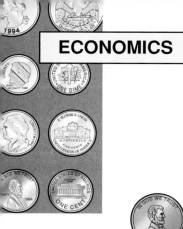

Introducing The Lesson:

Write "Wish List" on the chalkboard. Ask students if they know what type of items would appear on such a list. Confirm that wish lists name things that we would like to have. Then ask students to name things that they have wished for. Record responses on the chalkboard.

Steps:

1. After all students have had the opportunity to respond, ask them to identify ways to get the things they wish for. Acknowledge that sometimes we get these things as presents but that most often people work to earn money for the things they would like to have. Then share the Background Information on page 87.

2. Next write "Ways To Earn Money" on the chalkboard. Have students name chores or jobs they might do to earn money. List these responses on the chalkboard.

3. Distribute a copy of page 89 to each student. Explain that the newspaper pictured at the top contains information about an entertainment park. It also shows a list of jobs available.

4. Review the directions for completing the paper. Then have each child complete it independently.

5. Challenge students to complete the Bonus Box activity.

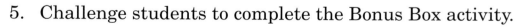

Wish List	Ways To Earn Money
skates	take out trash
video game	clean the garage
basketball	wash dishes
camera	do yard work

Explaining uses of money as a means of exchange

The World Of Work

Read the newspaper pages below.
Make a wish list of things you would like to do at Fun Town.
Then make another list of ways to earn the money.

Entertainment Section

Now Open **FUN TOWN!**
Come see us for fun!

Movie ticket $3.00
Bowling $3.00
Video tokens $5.00
Face painting $2.00
Pizza & soda $4.00
Ice cream $1.00

Help-Wanted Section

Now hiring part-time help.

Wash dishes $1.00
Rake leaves $5.00
Weed garden $3.00
Sweep and mop .. $4.00
Walk the dog $2.00
Dust furniture $1.00
Fold laundry $2.00
Water plants $2.00

My Wish List	Cost	Ways To Earn Money	Payment
_____	_____	_____	_____
_____	_____	_____	_____
_____	_____	_____	_____
_____	_____	_____	_____
_____	_____	_____	_____
_____	_____	_____	_____
Total $ _____		**Total** $ _____	

Bonus Box: On the back of this paper, write about something you would like to have. Then explain how you could earn the money for it.

How To Extend The Lesson:

- Bring in an assortment of U.S. coins and currency for students to examine. Ask students to look for markings or features that make each denomination unique. Work as a class to make a chart listing each coin or bill, its value, and its distinguishing features. Then have students illustrate different coins and bills. (Some students may illustrate the same coin or bill.) Display the drawings and the chart on a bulletin board titled "Show Me The Money!"

- Send your students on a shopping trip without leaving the classroom. Organize the children into groups of four. Give each group a shopping list of five items and several sales circulars. Challenge each group to search the circulars for the best price on each item. After an appropriate amount of time, initiate a classroom discussion about the results of their bargain hunting.

- Reinforce students' understanding of making purchases with this activity. Give each student $20.00 in duplicated play money. Provide catalogs for students to look through for "purchases" they would like to make. Have each child write down what he would like to buy, why he wants it, and how much it will cost. Then have him total his purchases and attach the play money needed for his expenditures. Provide time for each student to discuss how much money he spent, the types of purchases he made, and what he plans to do with the remainder.

I'd Like:	Why:	Cost:
toy dog	sister's b-day	$2.00
toy camera	take pictures	$3.00
gum	blowing bubbles	$1.00
soccer ball	playing soccer	$2.00
video game	give to brother	$10.00
	Total	$18.00

- Arrange a field trip to a bank to see how money is deposited and withdrawn, how it can be borrowed, and the different types of savings plans that are available. Also arrange for a bank employee to answer questions that students have prepared in advance. If possible, ask the bank to provide take-home information about savings programs for children.

The Flower Factory

*Student understanding of division of labor will bloom
with this cooperative activity!*

Skill: Participating in a division-of-labor activity

Estimated Lesson Time: 30 minutes

Teacher Preparation:
Duplicate page 93 for each student.

Materials:
1 copy of page 93 per student
crayons
scissors
glue

Background Information:

People working together in communities help one another meet
their needs for food, clothing, shelter, love, and safety. *Division of
labor*—dividing work so that each person has a special job—
produces more and better services for the same amount of work.
With a division of labor, no one has to do all the work. For example,
to make clothing we divide the labor. One group of people grows
cotton, another makes thread out of the cotton, another turns the
thread into fabric, and another fashions the fabric into a garment.
People in communities share their work to save time.

Introducing The Lesson:

Begin the lesson by drawing a simple barn, chicken, and cornfield on the chalkboard. Ask students to name other items that can be found on a farm. List their responses on the chalkboard.

Steps:

1. After students have named several items, point out that a farm has almost everything a family needs to survive. Have students offer examples of needs that can be met with the resources on a farm.

2. Point out that many people no longer live on farms. Ask students how these people's needs are met. Reinforce that many people buy the things they need with money that they make from their jobs. Explain that instead of families working on farms to produce all their resources, we now have communities that divide the labor. Explain the Background Information on page 91.

3. Ask students to name different types of jobs in the community, such as a teacher, a baker, and a firefighter. Have the students identify the community's wants and needs that are met by having everyone contribute their skills to the workforce.

4. Tell students that they are going to work together to make a classroom bouquet. Each student in a group will be assigned one part of a flower to complete. Tell students that the labor will be divided so that each student can concentrate on his part of the job.

5. Place students in groups of four. Distribute a copy of page 93 to each child. Assign each group member a number that corresponds with one of the jobs listed on the page.

6. Provide time for each group to complete its flower. Allow time for discussion about how each group worked together to complete the job.

7. Collect the projects and display them as a classroom bouquet. If desired, present each student with a copy of the award pattern on page 94.

The Flower Factory

Your teacher will assign you a number.
Follow the directions for your number.

Worker 1: Your job is to cut the page on the dotted lines.
Give the piece with the **petals** to **Worker 2**.
Give the piece with the **stem** to **Worker 3**.
Give the piece with the **center** to **Worker 4**.
Make sure everyone is doing his job.

Worker 2: Your job is to color and cut out the petals. When you have completed your job, give the petals to **Worker 4**.

Worker 3: Your job is to color and cut out the stem. When you have completed your job, give the stem to **Worker 4**.

Worker 4: Your job is to color and cut out the center. When the other workers have passed their pieces to you, glue them together to make a flower.

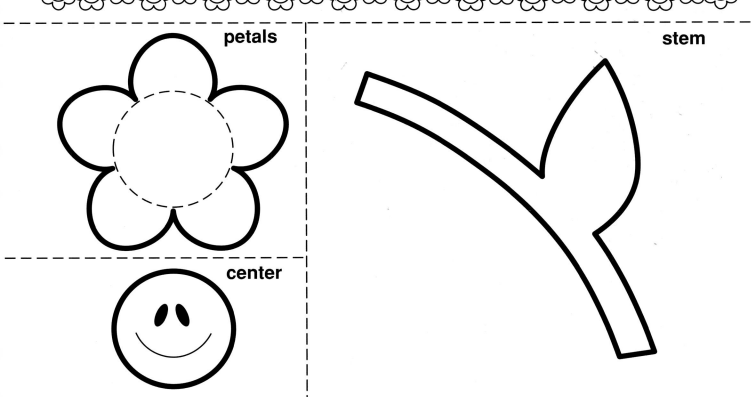

petals

stem

center

How To Extend The Lesson:

- Reinforce the concept that people in a community share work to help save time. Have each youngster illustrate one way people in his community share work, such as a farmer growing food that a grocer sells. Then instruct him to write a sentence or two that explains his illustration. Collect the papers and display them on a bulletin board titled "Sharing The Work!"

- Explain to students that keeping people safe in a community is a division of labor. Encourage youngsters to brainstorm emergency situations in which community members depend upon one another for help, such as when a rising river causes flooding or there is a widespread blackout. List student responses on the chalkboard. Then divide students into small groups. Have each group select a different situation from the list. Then instruct group members to determine how citizens work together to keep the community safe during its selected emergency.

- Invite parents or community members to visit the classroom and discuss their jobs. In advance, ask each guest to explain to students how they are part of a division of labor and how they need to count on others as well as be accountable to others. After each guest leaves, invite students to role-play some of the community workers at their jobs.

Award

Many Thanks
to you and your team
for a
job well done!

©1999 The Education Center, Inc. • *Lifesaver Lessons®* • TEC514

Answer Keys

Page 65
1. true
2. false
3. true
4. false
5. true
6. true
7. false
8. true
9. true
10. false
11. true
It is a sewing machine!

Page 73
Food/Water:
granola bar
water
trail mix

Clothing:
hat
hiking boots
jacket

Shelter:
tent
Bonus Box: Answers will vary.

Page 85
(Reasons will vary.)
1. purple   A farmer sells his crops.
2. green   Parents buy household items.
3. purple   He is a person who makes and sells TVs.
4. purple   She provides a service.
5. green   She buys game tickets and sports equipment.
6. purple   He provides a service.
7. green   He is a shopper.
8. green   She buys airline tickets, souvenirs, and meals.

Bonus Box: Answers will vary.

Grade 2 Social Studies Management Checklist

SKILLS	PAGES	DATE(S) USED	COMMENTS
COMMUNITIES			
The Family	3		
Community Helpers	7		
Urban, Suburban, And Rural Settings	11		
GOVERNMENT & CITIZENSHIP			
Rules In A Neighborhood	15		
Good Neighborhood Citizens	19		
Neighborhood Rights	23		
Democratic Decision Making	27		
U.S. Symbols	31		
MAP SKILLS			
Maps And Globes	35		
Cardinal Directions	39		
Reading A Map Key	43		
Geographic Terms	47		
OUR NEIGHBORS			
Neighbors Around The World	51		
Holidays From Different Cultures	55		
HISTORY			
Timeline Of U.S. Holidays	59		
Comparing Today With The Past	63		
Historical Figures	67		
ECONOMICS			
Wants And Needs	71		
Supply And Demand	75		
Goods And Services	79		
Producers And Consumers	83		
Money As A Means Of Exchange	87		
Division Of Labor	91		